3.95

D1196427

# SACRAMENTS OF HEALING AND OF VOCATION

FOUNDATIONS OF CATHOLIC THEOLOGY SERIES

Gerard S. Sloyan, *Editor*

# SACRAMENTS OF HEALING AND OF VOCATION

PAUL F. PALMER, SJ

*Alma College*
*Los Gatos, California*

PRENTICE-HALL, INC.
*Englewood Cliffs, N.J.*

1963

*Imprimi potest:*

John J. McGinty, SJ
Provincial, New York Province

*Nihil obstat:*

James F. Magner, SS, STD
Censor Librorum

*Imprimatur:*

Thomas J. Bowe, JCD,
Vicar General of the Archdiocese of San Francisco
October 16, 1962

 *Library of Congress Catalog Card No.: 63-10939*



PRENTICE-HALL INTERNATIONAL, INC., *London*
PRENTICE-HALL OF AUSTRALIA, PTY., LTD., *Sydney*
PRENTICE-HALL OF CANADA, LTD., *Toronto*
PRENTICE-HALL FRANCE, S.A.R.L., *Paris*
PRENTICE-HALL OF JAPAN, INC., *Tokyo*
PRENTICE-HALL DE MEXICO, S.A., *Mexico City*

C

# EDITOR'S NOTE

This series offers the depth and richness of the divine message of salvation proclaimed to us by Christ. The theology, or "faith seeking understanding," contained here is not on a catechetical level, nor yet on a complex, higher level; it is clear and nontechnical, but at the same time adult and thorough. It is a scholarly presentation of revelation.

These volumes do not adopt an apologetic approach. They

neither attempt to justify Catholic faith nor aim at convincing those who do not profess it of the reasonableness of believing. This series is written primarily for those who already believe, who accept the Church as the living continuation of Christ, and the Scriptures as divinely inspired.

The authors do not attempt a philosophy of God or of Christianity, but a study of the mystery of God seen through the eyes of faith. The mystery of faith will not be dispelled by the study of these books. It will remain.

Since some background in philosophy on the part of the reader is needed, and cannot in every case be presumed, there are times when philosophical terms will need to be explained. Philosophical reasoning is very much a part of speculative theology.

Although the breakdown of the series is along traditional lines, each volume is designed to emphasize the oneness of God's plan of salvation and not its different facets. Distinction is made in order to unite. What is taught in the Scriptures is stressed, so that it may be seen how men of the Bible understood the message entrusted to them. The historical aspects of doctrine as held by Christians are then treated: the testimony of the early Christian writers and the liturgy to the belief of the Church; the controversies and heresies that necessitated defense and precise formulation, and finally, the magisterial teaching in each subject area. In this way speculative theology, or the present understanding of each mystery, is not seen in isolation from the sources of faith.

Thus, the revealed Christian message is viewed as the *tradition* (in the fullest and best sense of that theological term) expressed in and through the Church over the centuries—more explicitly formulated, from age to age, and with further applications. But it is still the same saving message begun in the Old Testament and perfected in the mystery and person of Jesus Christ.

One last point is important. Although the study of theology is an exercise of intellect, it can never be exclusively this. The message of Jesus Christ is a living Word, an invitation to participate in the saving event of the redemption, starting in this world by faith and the union of grace, and culminating in heaven by vision and immediate union. This invitation demands response or living faith. The study of the Christian message through theology requires such response, for the message is not something that was heard and assented to once. It is a Word addressed to us that requires our vigorous "Yes" for a lifetime.

# CONTENTS

## PART ONE—THE SACRAMENTS OF HEALING


CHAPTER ONE

THE SACRAMENT OF PENANCE, *page* 5

*New Testament background. Early controversies. Description of early discipline. The Celtic and the Continental discipline. Belief of the early Church. Scholastic teaching on the sacrament. The Reformation and Trent. From Trent to the present. The effects of penance.*

A SUPPLEMENT—INDULGENCES

CHAPTER TWO

THE SACRAMENT OF EXTREME UNCTION, *page* 42

*The ministry of healing in the New Testament. Early evidence for rite of anointing the sick. Scholastic speculation. The Reformation and Trent. Recent contributions.*

PART TWO—THE SACRAMENTS OF VOCATION

CHAPTER THREE

THE SACRAMENT OF ORDER, *page* 55

*The New Testament witness. Early development of orders. Early heresies. The Middle Ages. The Reformation and Trent. More recent questions. The power and grace of order.*

A SUPPLEMENT—PRIESTLY CELIBACY

CHAPTER FOUR

THE SACRAMENT OF MARRIAGE, *page 78*

*Marriage in the Old Testament. Marriage in the New Testament. Early controversies. Marriage as a sacrament. Sacrament and contract. The bond of marriage. The grace of marriage. The purpose of marriage. Marriage as a vocation.*

A SUPPLEMENT—THE RELIGIOUS LIFE

SELECTED READINGS, *page 109*

ABBREVIATIONS, *page 111*

INDEX, *page 113*

PART ONE

# THE SACRAMENTS OF HEALING

At Capharnaum Jesus not only cured a man of his paralysis, he cured him of his sins. The incident is related in Lk 5, 17–26, Mk 2,1–12, and Mt 9,1–8. A paralytic was lowered through an opening in the roof to the feet of Jesus. Seeing the faith of the paralytic's friends, Jesus said to him: "Son, your sins are forgiven." The scribes and pharisees who were present argued: "Who can forgive sins but God only?" Jesus replied:

"That you may know that the Son of Man has power on earth to forgive sins—he said to the paralytic—I say to you, arise, take up your pallet and go to your house." Mark and Luke recount the wonder of the crowd at the miracle they had witnessed. Matthew, with a likely reference to the "power on earth to forgive sins," concludes: "But when the crowd saw it they were struck with fear, and glorified God who had given such power to men." (Mt 9,8) The incident is important because of the light it throws on the sacraments of penance and extreme unction, healing sacraments of the Church.

/ In all three accounts of the miracle, the spiritual cure and the physical cure are intimately related. Jesus cured the paralytic to show his power over sin, but in doing so he also proved his power over physical infirmity, which is one of the effects of sin./This does not mean that all suffering and sickness are a punishment for personal sin or for the sins of one's parents (though the Jews of Jesus' time in fact thought so). It does mean that we are subject to sickness and death as a consequence of sin. Humanity suffers and dies because of Adam's sin. Because of that sin the whole of humanity stands in need of redemption: from original sin and its consequences, from personal sin and its consequences, consequences which affect both body and soul, mind and spirit. The purpose of the healing sacraments is to apply Christ's grace to those who have been regenerated through baptism and who still stand in need of his healing grace. The love they have for God through Christ has either been sundered or grown less fervent. It needs restoring to its pristine condition, or to the high point it had once reached through eucharistic life.

Although the physical miracle at Capharnaum was more striking than the spiritual cure, Jesus' critics were more shocked by his claim to forgive sins. Wonder workers had abounded in Old Testament times, but no judge or prophet had ever claimed to forgive sins. "Who can forgive sins, but God only"? Such was the objection raised by the scribes and the pharisees to Christ's claim to forgive sins as the Son of Man. Such is the objection to the Church's claim to forgive sins as the mystical body of Christ, as Christ continued in time. In a sense the objection is well made. Sin is an offense against God, and only God can pardon the offense. Sin involves the loss of supernatural life, and only God can restore that life to one who has forfeited it. Sin is an injury done to God through the abuse or misuse of his creatures, the self included. Only God can accept man's efforts to repair the injury. Sin is a violation of God's law, and only God can remit in part or cancel the debt of punishment incurred by such a violation. And yet, the objection fails to consider a principle which is basic to the Christian religion. Without denying that God is the Author of all forgiveness, whether of guilt or punishment, the principle states that God has entrusted to men the ministry of divine pardon. The principle finds its first expression in the sacred humanity of Christ, the visible organ or instrument of the godhead in reconciling man to God. The principle finds its continued expression in the Church, the visible instrument of the God-man, in reconciling man to God in Christ.

CHAPTER ONE

# THE SACRAMENT OF PENANCE

In 1551 the Council of Trent defined penance as a true and proper sacrament instituted by Christ for the purpose of reconciling the faithful to God as often as they fall into sin after baptism. (D911) Although the sacramental rite of penance is made up of the acts of the penitent—contrition, confession, and satisfaction—as well as the absolving action of the priest, the same council teaches that the power of the sacrament resides principally in the formula or words of the minister, "I absolve you. . . ." (D896) Accordingly, the effect of the sacrament of penance is ascribed principally, but not exclusively, to the power which the priest exercises in the sacrament. For this reason the treatise on the sacrament of penance usually begins with the question of whether Christ actually conferred on his apostles and their successors in the priesthood the power to forgive sins in the rite of penance. In keeping with the principle already stated of human instrumentality in the work of forgiveness, our inquiry begins with Christ's ministry of merciful love, since it is Christ's ministry which is continued in the Church.

## NEW TESTAMENT BACKGROUND

### *Christ's Ministry of Forgiveness*

As the Son of God, Christ could have forgiven sins on his own authority. Yet this would go counter to all we know from the New Testament revelation of his role as the servant of the Lord and minister in the heavenly sanctuary (Heb 8,2), even in his glorified state. In the case of the paralytic, Christ forgave sins as the Son of Man, as one sent by God, as God's representative, with power derived from God. (Cf. Lk 5,24.) As already noted, Christ's critics were shocked by his claim to forgive sins. The prophets had preached repentance unto the remission of sins. The priests of the Old Law had offered sacrifices for their own sins and for the sins of the people. At times a prophet might assure the sinner that his sins were forgiven. Thus, Nathan the prophet first accused David the king of the multiple crime of adultery and murder, and after receiving David's sorrowful admission of guilt, Nathan assured David that God had taken away his sins. (Cf. 2 Sm 12,13.) John the Baptist, the last of the prophets but Jesus, had also preached repentance, and after a confession of sins he baptized his converts with water "for repentance." (Mt 3,6.11)[1] Jesus too had preached repentance and had commissioned his apostles to do the same. But in the case of the paralytic he does not simply preach repentance, nor does he merely assure the the paralytic that he has been pardoned by God. Instead, he actually forgives the paralytic with a power which he has received from on high. "But that you may know that the Son of Man has power on earth



[1] A period between verse numbers indicates that the verses cited are successive but nonconsecutive.

to forgive sins"—he said to the paralytic—"I say to you, arise, take up your pallet and go to your house." (Lk 5,24)

## *The Apostolic Ministry of Forgiveness*

There is no scriptural evidence that any of the apostles other than St. Paul exercised the authority of forgiving sins in his own person apart from the sacrament of baptism. There are, however, two passages in the New Testament which support the Church's claim that Christ entrusted to the apostles the power or authority of forgiving sins. In Mt 18,18, the power to forgive sins is promised in the formula of binding and loosing. In Jn 20,23, the power is conferred in the formula of forgiving and retaining sins. Both texts are appealed to by the Fathers of the Church to justify the right which priests possess to forgive sins in the sacrament of penance. The Council of Trent (1545–1563) appealed to the text of John as the moment when Christ principally instituted the sacrament of penance.

### BINDING AND LOOSING

> But if your brother sin against you, go and show him his fault, between you and him alone. If he listens to you, you have won your brother. But if he does not listen to you, take with you one or two more so that on the word of two or three witnesses every word may be confirmed. And if he refuse to hear them, appeal to the Church, but if he refuse to hear even the Church, let him be to you as the heathen and the publican. Amen I say to you, whatever you bind on earth shall be bound also in heaven; and whatever you loose on earth shall be loosed also in heaven. (Mt 18,15–18)

At first glance there seems to be nothing more at issue in this passage than a simple dispute between two followers of Christ. However, such a dispute is made the occasion for introducing the role of the Church in the matter of sins. If the guilty party prove recalcitrant or impenitent, he is to be excommunicated. This is the meaning, according to most authors today, of the phrase "to bind." The Church binds by excommunicating the sinner. She looses by reconciling the sinner to the Church and to God. In other words, whom the Church excludes from the kingdom of God on earth, the same is excluded from the kingdom of God in heaven. Whom the Church reconciles to herself, God reconciles to himself. Obviously, God's confirmation of this action of the Church will be conditioned by the guilt and penitence of the sinner. In an earlier passage (Mt 16,19) the power of binding and loosing was promised to Peter in the context of the keys: "And I will give you the keys of the kingdom of heaven; and whatever you shall bind on earth shall be bound in heaven; and whatever you shall loose on earth shall be loosed in heaven." Because of this passage, Christian tradition will refer to the sacramental power of forgiving sins as the "power of the keys."

FORGIVING AND RETAINING

The disciples therefore rejoiced at the sight of the Lord. He said to them again, "Peace be to you! As the Father has sent me, I also send you." When he had said this, he breathed upon them, and said to them, "Receive the Holy Spirit; whose sins you shall forgive, they are forgiven them; and whose sins you shall retain, they are retained." (Jn 20,20–23)

Although some few Fathers of the Church cite this text to prove that sins are forgiven in baptism through the Holy Spirit, there is nothing in the text or context which would warrant the restriction of this passage to the sacrament of baptism. The Fathers of the Church generally, and the Council of Trent in particular, appeal to this passage to show that the power of forgiving sins extends to sins committed after baptism. And this is in keeping with the general tenor of Christ's words, which literally should read, "the sins of whomsoever you forgive, they are forgiven them." It should be noted, again, that the action of the Church in forgiving is confirmed by the action of God. In other words, whom the Church through her ministers—here the apostles—forgives, God forgives.

Thus, the Church's pardon through the ministry of those whose commission it is to continue the mission of Christ is the pledge, the earnest, the sign, or, if you will, the sacrament of divine pardon. Reconciliation with the Church is the external and efficacious sign of the invisible reconciliation which is effected between God and the sinner. In the early centuries of the Church, the climax of the sacrament of penance was frequently referred to as "peace and communion with the Church—*pax et communio.*" Thus, St. Augustine can say: "The peace of the Church forgives sins, and separation from the Church's peace retains sins." (*On Baptism, Against the Donatists,* 3,18,23)

EXCOMMUNICATION AND RECONCILIATION The practice of the early Church follows a pattern which is set by St. Paul in his two letters to the Corinthians. The sinner is first cut off from communion with the Church and, after a period of penance, he is reconciled again. Thus the

Church exercises her twofold power of binding or retaining by excommunicating the sinner, and of loosing or forgiving by reconciling the penitent. In 1 Corinthians we are introduced to a Christian who is guilty of an incestuous union. Paul writes: "I indeed, absent in body but present in spirit, have already, as though present, passed judgment in the name of our Lord Jesus Christ on the one who has so acted—you and my spirit gathered together with the power of our Lord Jesus—to deliver such a one over to Satan for the destruction of the flesh, that his spirit may be saved in the day of our Lord Jesus Christ." (1 Cor 5,3–5)

It has been argued that Paul's excommunication of the incestuous Corinthian was final, that the Church would no longer be interested in him, that grave sins of impurity were regarded as unpardonable in this life. In 2 Cor 12,21, however, Paul expresses the hope that those guilty of uncleanness and incontinence will have done penance before his arrival, an indication that penance and not outright exclusion was the punishment for those guilty of sins of the flesh. The action of Paul in 2 Corinthians is important because of the light it throws on the reconciliation of a sinner, whether he be the incestuous one of 1 Corinthians or not. In excommunicating the unfortunate Corinthian, Paul passed judgment "in the name of the Lord," and "with the power of our Lord Jesus." In reconciling a Corinthian, he does so "in the person of Christ." "Therefore I exhort you to assure him of your love for him. . . . Whom you pardon anything, I also pardon. Indeed, what I have forgiven—if I have forgiven anything—I have done for your sakes, in the person of Christ, that we may not be defeated by Satan; for we are not unaware of his devices." (2 Cor 2,8–11) Excommunication by way of penance will be the first step in the Church's discipline of penance; reconciliation by way of pardon will be the final act in the drama of forgiveness. Today, the Church does not ordinarily delay pardon. Penance usually *follows* the bishop's or priest's absolution. But in the Church of the first ten centuries, pardon was regarded as the fruit of penance. Except in an emergency, reconciliation normally followed a period of excommunication, but an excommunication which was medicinal and not terminal.

### *Unpardonable Sins?*

Although Christ's commission to forgive extends to the sins of "whomsoever," there are a number of texts in the New Testament which seem to limit the scope of forgiveness through the ministry of the Church. Thus, Christ himself speaks of a "sin against the Holy Spirit" which will be pardoned neither in this life nor in the world to come. (Cf. Mt

12,32.) St. John speaks of "sin unto death" for which Christians are not to pray. (1 Jn 5,16) The author of Hebrews admits the impossibility of "renewing unto repentance" those who have gone back to Judaism. (Heb 6,4–6) Yet besides Christ's own commission to forgive sins, which is couched in most general terms both in the promise to loose "whatsoever" and in the actual grant of power to forgive the sins "of whomsoever," there is another group of texts which holds out pardon to all who repent. Thus, St. John presumes that the newly baptized will never sin again: "Whoever is born of God does not commit sin; because his seed abides in him and he cannot sin, because he is born of God." (1 Jn 3,9) And yet earlier in the same epistle, John assures Christians: "If we acknowledge our sins, he is faithful and just to forgive our sins and to cleanse us from *all* iniquity." (1 Jn 1,9; emphasis added) Again, John relates in the Apocalypse that pardon upon repentance was promised the Christians of the Church of Thyatira who had been seduced by the woman Jezebel "to commit fornication, and to eat of things sacrificed to idols," and that Jezebel herself was given time to repent. (Ap 2,20–24) As already noted, St. Paul expected that those guilty of uncleanness and incontinence would have done penance before his return to Corinth. (Cf. 2 Cor 12,21.)

Non-Catholic historians of penance in general suggest that these seemingly conflicting passages represent a twofold tradition, one of harshness, the other of leniency. Catholic exegetes, on the other hand, see in the difficult passages not an unwillingness on the part of God or the Church to forgive the repentant sinner, but an obduracy of heart on the part of the sinner which precludes the possibility of pardon. Thus the sin against the Holy Spirit represents a deliberate closing of the eyes and a hardening of the heart to the striking advances of God through the miraculous intervention of the Holy Spirit. Catholic tradition, following the teaching of Pope Gelasius (492–496) has regarded the sin against the Holy Spirit as the sin of final impenitence. (Cf. *The Tome of Gelasius,* D167.) The sin unto death is not mortal sin as such but the sin of apostasy, a conscious rejection of Christ in whom alone there is life. So too, the author of the Epistle to the Hebrews has the sin of apostasy in mind when he speaks of the impossibility of "renewing unto repentance," those who had apostatized and returned to Judaism. For such "there remains no longer a sacrifice for sins, but a certain dreadful expectation of judgment." (Heb 10,26f)

## EARLY CONTROVERSIES

### *Correction or Rejection?*

One of the basic issues confronting the early Church was the question of her membership. Was she to regard herself, after the manner of the Essenes of the Qumrân community, as a select group drawn from the Jews, or, at least from gentiles who had first been circumcised? Would her members thus carefully selected be ejected outright if they failed to conform to her ethical standards? For a time St. Peter was reluctant to baptize the uncircumcised, a reluctance that was removed after the occurrence of a miracle which made it clear that Christianity was to be a universal religion embracing Jew and gentile. And at the Council of Jerusalem the universality of the Church's mission was proclaimed.

But what of those who failed to give the Christian witness by their lives? Was the Church, like certain religio-philosophical sects, to cut them off from membership irrevocably, or was she to try to save them? The New Testament teaching, as already seen, is somewhat obscure. Non-Catholic historians tend to see in that teaching a twofold tradition, one of rigorism, the other of leniency, and maintain that the spirit of exclusion and rigorism prevailed in the first two centuries. They argue that the early Church regarded herself as a community of saints in which sinful Christians were few, and who, if detected, were cut off entirely from the life of the community. In this way, so they say, the Church would keep herself without spot or blemish to greet the Lord on his coming.

There is little in the documents of the second century to substantiate the view of these historians. We have already seen that St. John in his Apocalypse holds out hope of pardon for Jezebel and her followers in the Church at Thyatira. And St. Polycarp, the disciple of St. John, instructs the presbyters at Philippi to be "compassionate and merciful toward all, turning back those who have gone astray." (*To the Philippians,* 6) Conversion, not exclusion, is the policy advocated by Polycarp. St. Paul, as we have already seen, expected the Corinthians to have done penance against his return to that city. A few decades later, Pope Clement of Rome invites the Corinthians to "intercede for those who have transgressed in any way," exhorting those who had instigated a schism in the Church of Corinth "to submit to the presbyters and to be corrected unto repentance." (*To the Corinthians,* 56,57) Once again, it is correction not rejection that is to be the policy toward grave sinners.

And yet there has always been a rigorist group within the Christian Church. Hermas, in the middle of the second century, wrote an allegorical treatise on penance called *The Shepherd* (*Pastor*). He tells us that there was a group at Rome who believed that there should be but one penance, the penance of baptism, and that those who stained their baptismal robes should have no second opportunity for penance. The shepherd, most likely the personification of the Church pastor or bishop, admits that sinlessness should be the ideal of the Christian. And yet the Lord, who is rich in mercy and who understands our weakness, has instituted a second penance and has entrusted it to the shepherd or bishop. (*Commandment* 4,4) Although for pastoral reasons *The Shepherd* takes a very dim view of penance that is often repeated, it does hold out hope of pardon after the performance of penance to the adulteress (*Commandment* 4,1) and to the apostate, provided he is not an apostate at heart but had denied Christ out of weakness during the time of persecution. (*Similitude* 9,26)

In the persecutions at Lyons and nearby Vienne in the year 177, Eusebius tells us that those who had apostatized were, at the intercession of the martyrs, "mothered anew, conceived anew, kindled to life anew." (*Ecclesiastical History*, 5,1) At the same time St. Irenaeus, the bishop of Lyons, informs us that in his day the Church did not hesitate to reconcile heretics and to receive certain female followers of Marcus, the Gnostic, who had been despoiled of their chastity as well as their faith. (*Against Heresies*, 1,13,5) Finally, in the opening decade of the third century Clement of Alexandria relates with approval the story of John the Evangelist who, as an old man, reconciled to the Church at Antioch a young convert who had become a robber chief and surpassed his fellows in the shedding of blood. (*Who Is the Rich Man That Is Saved?*, 42)

## *Montanism*

From these scattered instances, it is quite clear that the infant Church did not regard crimes such as apostasy, adultery, and murder as beyond the scope of ecclesiastical pardon. However, at the close of the second century a puritanical movement is found within the churches of Asia and Phrygia. The leader of the movement is the itinerant prophet Montanus, assisted by the prophetesses Prisca and Maximilla. In its ascetical teaching, Montanism was harsh and intolerant. First marriages were at best tolerated but widows and widowers who contracted a second marriage were branded as adulterers, and the sin of adultery was the unpardonable sin. Montanism is best known in the West from the writings of Tertullian of Carthage, its most fanatical disciple (d. 230?).

Tertullian wrote two treatises on penance. In the first *De Paenitentia* (*On Penance*) he writes as a Catholic and holds out hope of pardon to all classes of sinners. In the *De Pudicitia* (*On Modesty*), written as a Montanist, he admits that lesser sins can be forgiven by the bishop but, reversing his earlier position, insists that the sins of adultery, apostasy, and murder are "sins unto death," and hence unpardonable in this life. (*De Pudicitia,* 18,19) By way of reply, Tertullian's Catholic opponents appeal to Christ's parables of mercy, the lost sheep, the prodigal son; to Paul's reconciliation of the incestuous Corinthian; to the power granted by Christ to his apostles and their successors to forgive sins. (7–10, 13–17, 21) The controversy is important for the witness it gives to the Catholic claim that the bishop has power on earth to grant divine pardon.

## *Novatianism*

In the middle of the third century a new controversy centered on the question of reconciling apostates who had denied Christ in the persecution of Decius (250). After some hesitation, St. Cyprian of Carthage, who was forced to govern his church from exile, agreed that those who had apostatized and who had been recommended for pardon by those who had confessed the faith (martyrs) might be pardoned. He insisted however that the normal procedure of penance must be followed. This entailed a confession of sins, a period of penance, and the imposition of hands, normally by a bishop and his clergy, but in an emergency by a presbyter. Cyprian's action, which was paralleled by the Roman clergy and by Pope St. Cornelius, was challenged by Novatus of Carthage and by Novatian, a Roman presbyter who had ambitioned the papacy and, failing in his ambition, started his own sect, which lasted well into the fifth century. Like the Tertullianists, the Novatianists denied the Church's right to reconcile those guilty of such serious crimes as apostasy, murder, and adultery. Toward such, they taught, the Church could exercise her power of binding by excommunicating; she could not loose those whom she had bound.

## *The Council of Nicaea* (325)

The Montanists and the Novatianists were condemned as Puritans (*Cathari*) at the first ecumenical Council of Nicaea. Should they return to the Church they must promise in writing "to conform and follow the doctrines of the Catholic and Apostolic Church; that is, to have fellowship both with digamists [twice married] and with those who have lapsed in the persecution, for whom as well a time has been fixed and an occasion [for reconciliation] has been determined." (*Mansi*, 2,672, Can. 8) Of equal importance for the history of penance is the prescription of the Council that penitents are to be reconciled and granted viaticum at the time of death, a prescription which underscores the importance of the Church's mediation rather than the unaided efforts of the penitent. Even more important for future development is the concluding statement that "with regard to all, whoever they be, who are departing this life and who ask to partake of the eucharist, let the bishop, after investigation, grant it." (Can. 13) The rule of a single penance for those who had become public penitents will continue in the Church for another hundred years or more, but there was nothing to prevent a bishop in accord with Nicaea from reconciling a relapsed penitent ("recidivist") on his deathbed. True, the recidivist could not expect to rejoin the public penitents and have the Church publicly intercede for pardon—such a course would shock the catechumens—but there was nothing to prevent his reconciliation at the moment of death.

## DESCRIPTION OF EARLY DISCIPLINE

The discipline of penance is not everywhere uniform but it follows the general pattern set by Paul of excommunicating those guilty of grave crimes and later of reconciling them to the Church. We shall consider, in order, the sinner's confession, his sorrow or contrition, his penance or period of satisfaction, and lastly his reconciliation or absolution.

### *Confession*

As today, the first act in the drama of divine forgiveness was confession. In fact, the Greek word *exomologēsis* (confession) is referred to by Tertullian as a general term to express the acts of the penitent leading up to pardon. In the case of secret sins, the confession was voluntary and, as such, merited a shorter period of penance. In the case of public crimes, the sinner could be forced to acknowledge the charges brought against him. The confession was first made in secret to the bishop, or, in the more populous Churches of Rome, Antioch, and

Constantinople, to a priest-penitentiary. The Greek historian Sozomen (c.450) tells us that "in seeking pardon it is necessary to confess the sin; and since from the beginning, the bishops decided, as is only right, that it was too much of a burden to announce one's sins as in a theater with the congregation of the Church as witness, they appointed for this purpose a presbyter, a man of the best refinement, a man silent and prudent." (*Ecclesiastical History,* 7,16) Whether penitents were obliged or even allowed, in the case of secret sins, to make known the sins for which they were doing penance is not certain. The very fact that they were public penitents, as Augustine informs his catchumens, is proof enough that they "have committed crimes, either adulteries, or other deeds of enormity." (*On the Creed for Catechumens,* 7,15) However, Pope Leo the Great (440–461) regards the local practice of reading from a chart the sins for which penance was being done as "a defiance of apostolic rule." The pontiff concludes: "For that confession is enough which is first offered to God and then to the priest as well, who is present to intercede for the sins of the penitents." (*Letter 168*)

### *Penance*

After confession, the penitent was enrolled as a public penitent if his sin was sufficiently grave and, particularly, if his sin was the cause of grave scandal. He was clothed in goat's hair to symbolize his separation from the sheep of the fold, and covered with ashes to symbolize Adam's expulsion from paradise, here the paradise of the Church on earth. Enrollment in the order of penitents and separation from the rest of the congregation during the liturgy was the usual punishment for those guilty of adultery, apostasy, or murder. Those guilty of other mortal sins, such as theft, absence from divine service, and, in some churches, fornication, were separated from the eucharist or holy communion for a shorter period of time, but were not forced to take their place with the public penitents. To this extent we can speak of a private penance even in the early Church, although the celebration of penance, like that of baptism and the other sacraments, extreme unction excepted, was usually public.

In the West there seems to have been but one grade of public penance which was modeled on the grade of catechumen. During the Sunday liturgy, the penitent was privileged to remain for the reading of the Scriptures and the bishop's homily. After the dismissal of the catechumens, he was the recipient of an imposition of the hand and the object of special prayers said over him by the bishop. After these prayers he was dismissed. He was not allowed to remain for the prayers of the faithful which immediately preceded the offertory, nor for the eucharistic prayer or sacrifice-action which followed. Besides these liturgical features of penance, the penitent was obliged to fast, to multiply his prayers, and to engage in almsgiving and other good works.

In the churches of Asia Minor those guilty of serious crimes, we learn from St. Basil, do not immediately qualify as penitents in the strict sense of the term. For example in Cappadocia, one guilty of wilful murder proceeds only by degrees to full communion with the Church. As a *mourner* he spends four years outside the church building, "asking the faithful as they enter to pray for him, and confessing his iniquity." For four years, as a *hearer,* he is permitted to listen to the Scriptures and the bishop's homily. For five years, as a *faller* or penitent, he remains prostrate while prayers are said over him by the bishop and the congregation; then he takes his leave, after the dismissal of the catechumens. For four additional years, as a *bystander,* "he will stand with the faithful but will not share in the offering. After completing these years, he will partake of the Holies [i.e., holy communion]." (*Letter 217 of St. Basil,* Can. 56) In the same canonical letter we find that the period of penance for adulterers was fifteen years, for fornicators [husbands who have relations with single women] seven years; for those guilty of theft, two years, if they are convicted; one year as a *bystander* if the theft is freely confessed. Basil adds, however, that these lengthy periods of penance can be shortened at the bishop's discretion, dependent upon the repentance of the sinner. In the Church of Syria, it would seem that the period of penance did not last more than several weeks. (Cf. *Didascalia Apostolorum,* 6.)

In the West, the period of penance normally lasted during the space of Lent. However to make up for this rather abbreviated discipline, public penitents even after their reconciliation were obliged to forego marriage, or if married, to abstain from marital relations. They were not permitted to engage in trade, to enter military service, or to attend public amusements. Failure to observe these after-penalties reduced the reconciled penitent to the status of *bystander.* He might remain for the offering of the eucharistic sacrifice, but he could not receive holy communion unless he was in danger of death. (Cf. Pope St. Siricius, *To Himerus,* 5; c. 390.) From Pope St. Leo the Great, however, we learn that many of these penalties or disabilities were waived, particularly those respecting marriage and the use of marriage. (*Letter 167*)

### *Contrition*

Contrition or sorrow of heart has always been a necessary condition for gaining divine pardon. The Fathers of the Church not infrequently liken the tears of the penitent to the waters of baptism, and, in an age which was more emotionally demonstrative than our own, often demanded manifestation of grief as a sign of true sorrow of heart. Thus, St. Cyprian of Carthage (251) relates that a local synod of that city decided "that those who do not do penance, nor give evidence of sorrow for their sins with wholehearted and manifest expression of grief, are to be restrained altogether from hope of communion and peace. . . ." (*Letter* 55, 23) In the same letter Cyprian makes it clear that the mere fear of death without true repentance is not enough for reconciling those who are dying. This does not mean that fear of death and judgment is not a good thing but that this fear must lead the sinner to sorrow and repentance of his sin. Thus, Pope Gregory the Great (590–604) demands that the priest shall not absolve until God has first quickened the sinner with the grace of compunction or sorrow; but he distinguishes between two kinds of compunction or sorrow: one which is born of fear, the other of love, "since it is one thing to flee punishment, another to seek reward. . . . Accordingly, there are two kinds of compunction: some weep from fear, while others in their sorrow are affected by love." (*On Ezechiel, Homily* 2, 10,20f) True, the purpose of the long public penance, including the grade of *mourner,* was to arouse in the penitent sorrow motivated by love. But the practice of reconciling sinners on their deathbed, without previous penance, suggests that the Church did not demand perfect sorrow or contrition as a condition for reconciling such sinners.

### *Reconciliation*

Pope Innocent I (402–417) informs us that "with regard to penitents who are doing penance for graver or for lesser sins, it is the clear practice of the Roman Church that they be forgiven on the Thursday before Easter, so long as no illness intervenes." (*Letter* 25) Although we have no details of the early ceremony of reconciliation from Innocent himself, the eighth century *Gelasian Sacramentary,* based on earlier Roman practice, tells us that the penitent was reconciled at the close of the Mass of Catechumens on Holy Thursday, after which he was privileged to make his offering and to receive holy communion. The

*Gelasian Sacramentary* does not mention an imposition of hands for reconciling penitents, but there is earlier evidence that a final imposition of hands by the bishop and the clergy was an important feature of the early rite of reconciliation in the churches of Africa, Syria, and Rome.

Of some importance is the witness of the *Gelasian Sacramentary* to the formula or prayer accompanying reconciliation. All the prayers are deprecatory in character, in that they express a prayer for forgiveness rather than a declaration of absolution. Thus, the bishop prays: "Bestow, we beseech you, O Lord, on this your servant, fruit worthy of penance, that by obtaining pardon for the sins he has admitted, he may be restored unharmed to your holy Church, from whose unity [*integritate*] he has strayed by sinning. Through the Lord. . . ." (*Gelasian Sacramentary,* 1,38) Although this formula of reconciliation is supplicatory, the Church had no doubt that supplication made through her priests was both necessary and efficacious. Thus, Leo the Great, with an obvious reference to the formula of reconciliation, writes: "These remedies of divine goodness have been so arranged that God's pardon cannot be gained except through the supplication of priests." (*Letter 108,* 2) Earlier, St. Cyprian had exhorted each one to confess his sin while still in the world, "while satisfaction and forgiveness granted through the priests is acceptable to God." (*On the Lapsed,* 29)

## THE CELTIC AND THE CONTINENTAL DISCIPLINE

Historians of penance are generally agreed that there is a marked difference between the development of penance in the churches of Ireland, Wales, and Britain, the area of the Celtic discipline, and the churches on the continent. In Ireland, Wales, and to a great extent in England, the discipline of penance was normally administered by the abbot and the priest members of the monastic community. Accordingly, in the penitential handbooks prepared for confessors there is little mention of reconciliation by the bishop and even less reference to any liturgical setting given to reconciliation. Except for those guilty of notorious crimes who were sent into exile, garbed as penitents and carrying nothing more formidable than a pilgrim's staff, the penitent was not a marked man. His penance was performed in private and it would seem that he was "reconciled to the altar" quite privately. Again, possibly as the result of monastic influence, repeated penance and confession out of devotion seem to have been introduced. In the case of serious sins, however, the penitent was not absolved or reconciled until he had performed his penance in whole or in part.

On the continent, the liturgical public penance remained the normal discipline for those guilty of more serious sins. By the middle of the ninth century, however, the principle, "public penance for public crimes, secret penance for secret sins," becomes the established rule. In the case of secret sins, the practice was gradually introduced of reconciling the sinner on the occasion of his confession, as is the practice today. By the beginning of the eleventh century, only public penitents were reconciled in the solemn Mass for Penitents on Holy Thursday. By the thirteenth century the public penance came to be regarded by many as wholly disciplinary and distinct from the sacrament of penance. Today it has yielded to the practice of excommunicating those guilty of stated crimes, an excommunication which is imposed by the bishop and which in some cases can be lifted by the confessor prior to sacramental absolution.

Of particular interest in the development of the rite of penance is the introduction of the absolution formula. Up until the medieval period, the word "absolution" was rarely used in connection with the sacrament of penance. When it was first introduced, the absolution formula, whether optative "May God absolve," or declarative "I absolve," referred to the relaxation of penalties and not to the remission of guilt. As such these absolution formulas were used for the dead as well as the living. When the absolution was granted in the context of the sacrament of penance, the absolution formula followed the prayer for forgiveness or reconciliation. Gradually, however, the absolution formula became the sacramental formula. From the time of St. Thomas onward, and owing to his influence, the present declarative formula "I absolve you from your sins in the name of the Father and of the Son and of the Holy Spirit" has become the formula in the Church of the West.

## BELIEF OF THE EARLY CHURCH

The first Christian to question the right of the Church to forgive serious sins was Tertullian, the Montanist (c. 220). He was willing to admit that the bishop could absolve from lesser sins, but when a Catholic bishop, either of Carthage or Rome, claimed that he was prepared to forgive those guilty of sins of the flesh after the due performance of penance, Tertullian challenged the claim by maintaining that God alone could forgive such sins, that Catholics in forgiving adulterers were usurping a power that belonged to God alone. Quite inconsistently, Tertullian admitted that the power of forgiving sins or the power of loosing was given to Peter, but to Peter alone and not to his successors in the priesthood. (Cf. *De Pudicitia,* 3,21.) In the middle of the same century Novatian denied the Church's right to absolve those guilty of apostasy, a denial that he ultimately extended to all serious sins. In rejecting the views of Tertullian and Novatian, the Church asserted her right to reconcile the sinner with God. She insisted that this power of forgiving sins, entrusted to Peter and the Apostles, was continued in her bishops and priests.

### *Penance as a Sacrament*

The sacramental nature of penance and, more particularly, of the priest's absolution is seen both in the practice and attitude of the Church as well as in the explicit statements of her Fathers. As already noted, the discipline of penance leading up to reconciliation was modeled on the discipline of the catechumenate leading up to baptism. In fact, penance is often referred to as a second and more laborious baptism. In the third century Syriac *Didascalia,* the bishop likens the effect of reconciliation through a laying on of the hand to the effect of baptism: "Whether by the imposition of the hand or by baptism they receive the communication of the Holy Spirit." (ch. 10) In a fragment from the writings of St. Athanasius (c. 370), we have the same parallel between baptism and penance: "Just as a man baptized by a human priest is illumined by the Holy Spirit, so also he who makes confession in penance receives through the priest forgiveness by the grace of God." (*PG* 26, 1316)

This explicit teaching of the Fathers is reflected in the attitude of the people toward penance and in the solicitude of the Church that serious sinners be reconciled before death or when in an emergency. Thus, during the Vandal invasion of North Africa, St. Augustine exhorts his clergy to remain at their posts. The reason he gives underscores both the sacramental character of penance and its necessity. "How great a crowd of both sexes and all ages is accustomed to gather in the Church, some demanding baptism, others reconciliation, others the discipline of penance itself, all seeking consolation and the administration of the sacraments. But if ministers are lacking, how great will be the destruction that follows those who leave this life either unregenerate or bound." (*Letter* 228, 8) Not only does Augustine refer to penance as a sacrament but he equates it with the sacrament of baptism, and teaches that the priest's reconciliation or loosing of the sinner is just as necessary for salvation as is the sacrament of baptism.

### *Necessity of Penance*

According to the Council of Trent, the sacrament of penance is just as necessary as the sacrament of baptism, a truth implied in the passage cited above from St. Augustine. There are, however, many explicit references to the necessity of penance and of sacramental confession in the early Church Fathers. Thus St. Cyprian exhorts the sinner to confess his sin "while his confession can still be received, while satisfaction and forgiveness granted through the priests is acceptable to God." (*On the Lapsed,* 28) Nor is this exhortation directed only to those who had publicly apostatized in the Decian persecution. Those who had even contemplated apostasy are expected "to confess this very thing to the priests of God." (*Ibid.,* 29) In the fourth century there were repeated warnings to those who put off penance, warnings which would be meaningless if the sinner were free to make his peace with God alone. To the sinner's objection: "I do penance in secret; before God I do it; the Lord who forgives knows that I do penance in my heart," Augustine's reply is not singular: "Was it then said without reason: 'Whatsoever you shall loose on earth shall be loosed in heaven?' Was it then without reason that the keys were given to the Church?" (*Sermon* 392)

In the East the catalogue of penances assigned for specific sins, some public, some secret, is evidence enough that the sinner did not have the option of confessing either to the priest or to God alone. The teaching of the East as well as the West is summed up by Leo the Great in the middle of the fifth century:

> God's pardon cannot be gained except through the supplication of priests. For the mediator of God and men, the man Christ Jesus, has passed on this power to those who are placed over the Church, that they may grant both the discipline of penance to those who confess . . . and admit the same through the door of reconciliation to fellowship in the sacraments." (*Letter 108,* 2)

## SCHOLASTIC TEACHING ON THE SACRAMENT

### *The Early Scholastics*

In the twelfth century, penance was numbered among the seven sacraments of the New Law. In the early part of the century, however, the sacrament was limited by many to the acts of the penitent: contrition, confession, and satisfaction. The absolution of the priest was regarded by many as remitting not so much the guilt of sin as the punishment due to sin. As already noted, absolution formulas were used for the dead as well as the living, and they were being used now in granting indulgences, a grant which presupposed that the guilt of sin was already removed. In this context, Peter Abelard (d.1140), in the first wave of scholastic teachers after Anselm, argued that the operative element in penance is true sorrow of heart which is motivated by love. Confession and satisfaction are necessary if the opportunity is present. (*Ethics,* 19,20) Abelard discusses the power of the keys, but only in the context of granting indulgences or in remitting something of the temporal punishment due to sin. (*Ethics,* 25)

Peter Lombard (d.1160) was the most influential of all the early scholastics. His four books of *Opinions* (*Libri Sententiarum*) will be commented upon by the great scholastic doctors well into the fourteenth century. Unfortunately, his teaching on the role of the priest in the sacrament of penance does not go much beyond that of Peter Abelard. The guilt of sin is forgiven by perfect sorrow alone. Although confession is necessary if a priest is available, the sin has already been forgiven through the grace of perfect sorrow. The role of the priest is to declare that the sinner has been forgiven by God, or to remit something of the punishment due to sin, or to reconcile the sinner to the Church if he has been excommunicated. (4 *Sent.*, 17,2; 18,6f) By this time, however, the older idea of reconciliation with the Church as the efficacious sign of reconciliation with God seems to have been lost.

Fortunately, the ideas of Abelard and Lombard were not unchallenged. Hugh of St. Victor (d.1142), Abelard's chief critic and opponent, insisted that the operative element in the sacrament of penance was the power of the keys. Until the sinner was reconciled by the priest he was liable to eternal damnation. To the objection that only God can forgive sins, Hugh replies that this power was first entrusted to Christ in his humanity and then communicated by him to his apostles and their successors in the priesthood. The commission given is not to declare that sins are forgiven but: "Whose sins you shall forgive, they are forgiven." The penitent approaching the priest did not come, as the leper, to have the priest declare him clean. Rather he came seeking health. (*On the Sacraments*, 2,14)

The Abelard-Victorine debate lasted well into the thirteenth century. The disciples of Abelard, Peter Lombard included, insisted that perfect sorrow motivated by love was the indispensable disposition for divine pardon. The disciples of Hugh of St. Victor insisted that the absolution of the priest was the essential element in the divine drama of forgiveness. By this time, theologians were distinguishing between contrition, the disposition which alone gained pardon, and attrition, which was regarded by many as an imperfect and natural sorrow and not enough to gain pardon even when joined to the absolution of the priest. The first theologian to insist that attrition was good and the result of God's grace was William of Auvergne (d.1245). In his view, attrition or imperfect sorrow could be elevated in virtue of the priest's absolution. Accordingly, a person who approached the sacrament attrite could become contrite in and through the grace of the priest's absolution. Although William of Auvergne was not the author of the *dictum* ascribed to him, "*attritus fit contritus*," he represents a breakthrough in the impasse that perfect sorrow alone remits sins and that the action of the priest must be concerned with something other than the guilt of sin.

## *The Scholastic Doctors*

Out of deference to Peter Lombard, the Master of the Sentences, St. Bonaventure and St. Thomas admitted that sorrow informed or perfected by charity (contrition) should be the normal preparation for the priest's absolution. Both, however, admitted that a person who approached the priest with imperfect sorrow or attrition, provided he was in good faith, could be forgiven in and through the priest's absolution. Thus, putative contrition (attrition thought to be contrition) was sufficient preparation for the sacrament of penance. According to St. Thomas, the penitent who was only attrite on approaching the sacrament received through the priest's absolution the grace of contrition, which ultimately disposed him for pardon. Accordingly, the absolution of the priest was not the immediate cause of forgiveness. Rather the grace of absolution administered through the priest disposed the penitent for pardon which could be granted immediately only by God. (*Suppl.*, 18,1)

Of equal importance for the development of the sacramental rite of penance was the teaching of Thomas, based on Aristotelian notions, that the priest's absolution is the *form* of the sacrament of penance, giving a new value and efficacy to the acts of the penitent which Thomas referred to as the *matter* or quasi-matter of the sacrament. Accordingly, theologians should no longer speak of the acts of the penitent as the sacrament of penance and the absolution of the priest as an external concomitant. Rather the acts of the penitent informed by the priest's absolution constitute a single sacramental sign, a single sacrament. (*S. Th.*, 3,84,3) Against the Thomistic view of the sacrament, the Franciscan Scotus rebelled. Concerned, perhaps, with the overemphasis on the penitent's acts, he regarded the sacrament of penance as consisting solely in the absolution of the priest. The acts of the penitent were necessary, particularly contrition and confession, but they were necessary as conditions and not as inherent or constitutive parts of the sacramental rite or sign. (4 *Sent.*, 16,1,7) The Council of Trent discussed the acts of penitent and priest in the context of St. Thomas rather than in that of Scotus, but it did not condemn Scotus' view. There were larger issues at stake at the Council of Trent, and the Fathers of the Council could allow domestic disputes to work themselves out in continuing scholastic dialogue.

## THE REFORMATION AND TRENT

### *Luther, Calvin, and Cranmer*

Martin Luther's personal experience as a monk of St. Augustine colors his teaching not only on the sacrament of penance but on the whole sacramental system. Scrupulous by temperament, Luther wanted personal assurance that his sins were forgiven. This assurance he found neither in his own acts of sorrow nor in the fulfillment of the penances imposed by his confessor. Absolved, he still felt that he was a sinner. Concupiscence or the rebellious tendencies of the flesh were uprooted neither by his own efforts nor by the priest's absolution. He concluded, therefore, that man must, as a result of the fall, always remain essentially a sinner. And yet, for some time after his excommunication by Pope Leo X (1520), he continued to regard penance along with baptism and the Lord's supper as a sacrament of the New Law. The purpose of the sacrament, however, was not to remove man's sinfulness or guilt. At most, the priest could assure the sinner of God's willingness to overlook his sinfulness, and to substitute for his sinfulness the sinlessness of

Christ. In absolving him, the priest could assure him that Christ shielded him from the Father's wrath, that his sinfulness, although present, would in virtue of Christ's saving death no longer be imputed to him or laid to his account.

Luther admitted two parts of penance: contrition, or the fear of a terrified conscience prompted by God's threatening words of condemnation for the sinner, and confidence, or faith in God's mercy and readiness to spare the sinner. This response of confidence, or faith in God's promise to save, is first made in baptism; it is recalled by the priest's absolution in the sacrament of penance. Actually, the role of the priest or minister in all the sacraments is to give graphic expression through word and symbol to the gospel of mercy, and thus to engender or renew faith (confidence) by which man alone is justified or made righteous. It mattered little whether the priest absolved in jest. It mattered only that the sinner believed in all confidence and faith that his sins were forgiven.

Luther had at times experienced this personal assurance in the sacrament of penance, and he was anxious that confession of sins to a priest or minister should continue among his followers. To this end he drew up in his *Short Catechism* an instruction on how "simple folk" are to confess and be absolved. At the close of the confession, which is somewhat detailed but quite reticent on sins against the sixth and ninth commandments, the priest or minister is advised to use the declarative formula, "I absolve you of your sins. . . ." as used at the time by Catholics. At this point we might observe that there are some Lutheran groups today who feel that the general confession and the absolution given in their liturgy are not enough to arouse in sinners sufficient faith or confidence, and hence are reintroducing the practice of private confession to an ordained minister.

Missing from Luther's instruction on confession is all reference to sorrow for sin and to a penance to be imposed by the confessor. This is in keeping with Luther's general teaching that the acts of the penitent—apart from faith and confidence—contribute nothing to sin's forgiveness. Again, to ask the sinner to expiate or make satisfaction for his sins by acts of penance would imply that something was wanting in Christ's satisfaction for our sins on Calvary.

John Calvin, leader of the reform movement at Geneva, accepted Luther's teaching on the role of faith or confidence in the sacraments. Like Luther he admitted the psychological value of confession to a minister of the gospel, particularly by those who are troubled in conscience, but he denied that penance was a sacrament instituted by Christ. Calvin made so little of private confession that it has long ceased to be practiced among Presbyterians and, with the exception of a few small groups in France, by Calvinists and other Reformed Protestants.

Thomas Cranmer, archbishop of Canterbury, was the leader of the reform movement in the Church of England. Borrowing from Lutheran and Calvinist sources, he limited the sacraments of the New Law to baptism and the Lord's supper. However, he retained in the rite for visiting the sick the practice of confession to a priest, if the sick person "feels his conscience troubled with any weighty matter." After this confession the priest is to absolve him, using the now traditional formula, "I absolve you from all your sins. In the name of the Father. . . ." (*Book of Common Prayer*, 1552) With the exception of Anglo-Catholics, who regard penance as a sacrament, private confession is rarely practiced by Anglicans and Episcopalians in time of health.

## *The Synthesis of Trent*

The sacrament of penance is discussed in the fourteenth session of the Council of Trent (1551). The doctrinal decree runs to nine chapters and is followed by fifteen canons which sum up and anathematize as heretical the errors of the Protestant Reformers. Following the order of the canons and inserting, where advisable, further clarification from the doctrinal decree, we offer the following summary of Trent's teaching. (Cf. D894–925.)

INSTITUTION AND PURPOSE 1. Penance is a true and proper sacrament instituted by Christ our Lord for reconciling the faithful to God as often as they fall into sin after baptism. (Can. 1) The sacrament was principally instituted after the Lord's resurrection when he entrusted to the apostles and their legitimate successors the power of forgiving sins, for the purpose of reconciling those who had fallen after baptism. (ch. 1)

BAPTISM AND PENANCE: THEIR NECESSITY 2. Penance is a distinct sacrament from baptism. (Can. 2) It differs from baptism in matter and form, and in the fact that it can be given only to those over whom the Church has jurisdiction. Penance, after all, includes a judgment of Christ, through the Church, on those who have freely submitted themselves to this judgment. Through baptism a person obtains the full and complete remission of sins, whereas in penance which has been called "a laborious baptism" complete remission is had only after many tears and strivings of our own. "And yet, this sacrament of penance is just as necessary for salvation in the case of those who have fallen after baptism as is baptism itself for such as have not as yet been regenerated." (ch. 2)

MEANING OF WORDS OF INSTITUTION 3. The words of the Lord: "Receive the Holy Spirit, whose sins you shall forgive . . ." are to be understood of the power of forgiving and retaining sins in the sacrament of penance, as the Catholic Church has always understood them from the beginning. They are not to be twisted to mean the power of preaching the gospel. (Can. 3 and ch. 1)

PARTS AND EFFECT OF SACRAMENT 4. For the integral and complete remission of sins three acts are required of the penitent, the quasi-matter of the sacrament, namely, contrition, confession, and satisfaction. It is heretical to say that there are but two parts of penance, namely the terrors of a stricken conscience, and faith conceived from the gospel or from the absolution, whereby one believes that his sins are forgiven him through Christ. (Can. 4) The form of the sacrament, "wherein the power of the sacrament chiefly resides," consists of the words of the minister: "I absolve you. . . ." The reality (*res*) signified by the sacrament and its effect is reconciliation with God, although there is likely to follow also at times peace and serenity of conscience, accompanied by an overwhelming consolation of spirit. (ch. 3)

CONTRITION 5. Contrition, which is prepared for by the consideration of the abhorrence of sin, the loss of eternal happiness, and the incurring of eternal damnation, along with the resolve to better one's life, is true and profitable sorrow and prepares a man for grace. Again, such sorrow is free and voluntary and not wrung from a man. (Can. 5) Contrition is defined as "sorrow of soul and detestation of sin committed, with the resolve not to sin again." Such contrition has been necessary in every age to gain pardon for sin, and, in the case of one who has fallen after baptism it prepares for the remission of sin "provided it is joined with confidence in the divine mercy." This contrition involves not only the resolve to begin life anew but also an "abhorrence" of one's former life, as passages from Ezechiel (18,31), from the Psalms of David (50[51],6; 6,7), and from Isaia (38,15) bear witness. (ch. 4)

PERFECT AND IMPERFECT CONTRITION This contrition or sorrow of heart is at times perfected by charity and reconciles a man to God before the actual reception of the sacrament, so long as it is accompanied by the intention of receiving the sacrament, an intention which is included in perfect contrition. Imperfect contrition or attrition "is ordinarily conceived from a consideration of sin's malice, or from fear of hell and punishment." Provided it excludes the will to sin and is accompanied by hope of pardon, it is a gift of God and prepares for justification, insofar as it "disposes him for the attainment of God's grace in the sacrament of penance." Accordingly, it is a calumny to say that Catholics have taught that the sacrament of penance confers grace without any good disposition on the part of those who receive it. (ch. 4)

CONFESSION 6. Sacramental confession was instituted as necessary for salvation by divine law. The method of confessing to a priest in private has been observed from the beginning and is in accord with Christ's institution and command. (Can. 6) Confession is necessary, since Christ left priests to represent him as presiding judges. These would be unable to pass judgment without a knowledge of the case or to impose penances with equity. (ch. 5)

7. It is necessary by divine precept to confess each and every mortal sin one recalls after due and diligent reflection, along with the circumstances which change the species of the sin. (Can. 7) Although venial sins may with due profit be mentioned in confession, they can be expiated by many other means. (ch. 5)

8. Confession [of mortal sins] is obligatory once a year, in conformity with the constitution of the fourth Lateran Council (1215). Accordingly the faithful are to be persuaded to confess during Lent. (Can. 8) The Lateran Council did not impose the obligation of confessing for the first time, but merely decided when the precept of confession should be observed [i.e., under pain of additional sin]. (ch. 5)

ABSOLUTION 9. The priest's absolution is a judicial act and not merely the ministry of declaring that sins are forgiven the penitent so long as the latter believes that he has been absolved, even though the priest absolves only in jest. (Can. 9 and ch. 6)

THE MINISTER 10. Priests are the sole ministers of absolution and they have the power of binding and loosing even though they themselves are in mortal sin. Accordingly, the power of binding and loosing, of forgiving and retaining sins, has not been given to each of the faithful, but to priests alone. (Can. 10 and ch. 6)



RESERVED SINS AND JURISDICTION 11. Bishops have the right to reserve cases to themselves, with the result that a priest is prevented from truly absolving in such cases. (Can. 11) Since a judicial process demands that sentence be passed only on those who are subjects, ordinary or subdelegated jurisdiction is required to absolve validly. All priests, however, can absolve penitents at the moment of death from every kind of sin and censure. No reservation has force at the moment of death. (ch. 7)

SATISFACTION 12. God does not always remit the entire punishment along with the guilt of sin, nor is the penitents' satisfaction merely a faith that Christ has satisfied for them. (Can. 12) That God does not always condone all punishment in forgiving the guilt of sin is clearly and strikingly exemplified in Sacred Scripture. (Cf. Gn 3,16ff; Nm 12,14ff; 20,11ff; 2 Sm 12,13ff, etc.) (ch. 8)

13. Satisfaction is made through the merits of Christ, by punishments which God inflicts or those enjoined by the priest, or those voluntarily undertaken, such as fasting, prayers, almsgiving, or other works of piety. Accordingly, the best penance is not simply a new life. (Can. 13)

14. The penitent's works of satisfaction are expressions of divine worship, which obscure neither the doctrine of grace nor the benefits of Christ's death. (Can. 14)

God's justice seems to demand more of the baptized who have violated the temple of God and who have grieved the Holy Spirit than of those who have sinned before baptism through ignorance. Again, the necessity of making satisfaction acts as a restraint for the future, whereas the actual performance of penance has the medicinal effect of healing the aftereffects of sin. Finally, in making satisfaction and in suffering for our sins, we become like to Christ who satisfied for our sins. For "if we suffer with him, we shall be glorified with him." (Rom 8,17) And yet it is in Christ that we make satisfaction, and it is from him that our works of satisfaction have their efficacy, and it is by him that they are offered to the Father, and it is through him that they are received by the Father. (ch. 8)

15. The purpose of the keys is not only to loose but also to bind. So, when priests impose penances they act in conformity with the purpose of the keys as instituted by Christ. Eternal punishment is taken away in virtue of the keys, but the debt of temporal punishment normally remains to be paid. (Can. 15)

Accordingly, the priest of the Lord, as the spirit of prudence shall suggest, ought to impose penances that "are salutary and suitable, proportioned alike to the nature of the sin and the ability of the penitent." These penances are designed not only as a remedy for weakness and a safeguard for a reform of life [medicinal] but as a vindication and punishment for past sins [vindicative]. (ch. 8)

### *Reflections on Trent*

Except for the condemnation of Peter Abelard, who suggested that bishops and priests were not given the same power as the apostles (*Council of Sens,* D379), the Church had not intervened in the prolonged scholastic debate on the efficacy of the priest's absolution and on the dispositions required of the penitent. Nor was it the purpose of Trent to settle domestic disputes. By insisting, however, that the purpose of the sacrament is to reconcile the sinner to God, and by teaching that the efficacy of the sacrament "chiefly resides" in the form of the sacrament, Trent put an end to all further discussion as to the effect of the priest's absolution. Again, in distinguishing between contrition which justifies the penitent before he receives the sacrament, and attrition which, even when motivated by fear of God's punishments, prepares for grace in the sacrament, Trent settled the qualms of earlier theologians who believed that putative contrition at least was necessary in one seeking sacramental pardon. Trent, however, did not clearly decide whether attrition from the motive of fear alone was a proximate preparation for grace in the sacrament, a point that will be debated in the years to come. (See p. 32.) Similarly, even though Trent adopts the terminology of St. Thomas in discussing the parts of the sacrament, the Thomist-Scotist debate on the matter and form of the sacrament was not settled.

In assessing the importance of Trent, it is well to note that the Fathers of the Council did not neglect the more experiential and subjective values prized so much by Protestants, such as the need of a vital faith and confidence in God's mercy toward the sinner. But Trent did insist on other acts or responses on the part of the penitent which were either neglected or denied by the Reformers, namely, a detailed confession of sins to the priest, true sorrow of heart, and a willingness on the part of the penitent to make amends for his sins. Unquestionably, God can cancel the debt of punishment in forgiving the sinner, and this he does through the sacrament of baptism. But the evidence from Scripture and from the practice of the early Church shows that even the reconciled sinner is called upon to expiate his sin.

Nor does this teaching of Trent lessen in any way the expiatory power of Christ's passion and death, as Protestants and many Eastern Orthodox theologians assert. Christ surely suffered and died for our sins, but we are not on that account freed of suffering and death which are the consequences of sin. The Christian solution to the problem is that given by Trent. It is because Christ suffered and died for our sins that there is expiatory value in our suffering and death, since it is in, from, by, and through Christ that our works of satisfaction have their efficacy. Climaxing the mystery of expiation is Trent's reminder that "in making satisfaction and in suffering for our sins, we become like to Christ who satisfied for our sins." "For if we suffer with him, we shall be glorified with him." (Rom 8,17)

## FROM TRENT TO THE PRESENT

### *The Orthodox Churches*

At the first reunion Council of Lyons (1274), a profession of faith in the seven sacraments was signed by the emperor Michael Palaeologus. Since that time Greek and Russian Orthodox theologians have agreed that penance has always been regarded in their own traditions as a true sacrament of the New Law, necessary for those who have sinned seriously after baptism. This faith of the Orthodox Churches is expressed in the Russian *Confession of Peter Moghila* (1640) and in the Greek *Confession of Dositheus,* which, together with the *Confession of Moghila,* was confirmed at the Council of Jerusalem (1672). Although Moghila's *Confession of Faith* speaks of the desire on the part of the penitent "to make satisfaction as assigned by the priest," most contemporary Orthodox theologians deny that the penalties imposed by the priest are designed to satisfy for sin. Rather, such penalties are wholly medicinal. Like the Protestants the Orthodox deny that any debt of punishment remains after the guilt of sin has been remitted, a denial which leads logically to the rejection of Catholic teaching on purgatory and the practice of granting indulgences.

### *The Jansenist Movement*

Jansenism was a rigorist movement within the Church. It received its name from Cornelius Jansen (*Jansenius*), successor to Michel du Bay (*Baius*) as professor of theology at the Catholic University of Louvain. The errors connected with the teaching of Jansen were condemned by Alexander VIII in 1690 and were revived at the heretical synod of Pistoia in 1794. Basic to Jansenist teaching on the subject of penance are the following propositions: (1) The Church should return to the primitive practice of excommunicating all serious sinners before absolving them and readmitting them to holy communion. (2) The priest should demand "fervor of charity" and "fervor in good works" before absolving a penitent. (3) Attrition from the motive of fear of hell is not a salutary act, since it does not exclude an affection for sin.

By way of reply, Catholic theologians argue: (1) The practice of absolving penitents before the fulfillment of penance does not affect the essential character of the sacrament of penance; even in the early Church sinners were absolved in an emergency before the completion or even the start of their penance. (2) Perfect charity, motivated by the love of God, even without the emotional overtone of "fervor," reconciles a sinner to God even before the sacrament is received. Hence perfect charity cannot be a necessary preparation for receiving the sacrament. (3) Fear is the beginning of wisdom and is frequently used in Sacred Scripture and by the Fathers of the Church as the prime motive for converting the sinner from his evil ways. So long as the fear is not completely self-regarding, or completely servile, the sinner will detest his sin as an offense against God, even though the motive for his repentance will be the fear of God's just punishments. True, such a motive is not prompted by love of God to the contempt of self, but neither is it prompted by love of self even to the contempt of God. The sinner does not positively reject all nobler motives for avoiding sin, but here and now realizes that the motive of fear is dominant—a fear, however, which is a gift of God and therefore salutary.

### *The Contritionist-Attritionist Controversy*

Unlike the Jansenists, the moderate contritionists admitted that sorrow for sin, motivated by fear, is a good act and the result of God's grace. But they denied that such attrition was a sufficient preparation for pardon even in the sacrament of penance. Perfect contrition, motivated by the fervor of charity, will reconcile the sinner outside the sacrament of penance, but in the sacrament imperfect contrition, motivated by some love of benevolence toward God (that is, loving him for himself and not merely for what he can do for the sinner), is necessary for the fruitful reception of the sacrament. The attritionists, many of them Jesuits and the most vigorous opponents of the Jansenists, appealed to the words of Trent in which attrition from the motive of fear is said to dispose the penitent "for the attainment of God's grace in the sacrament of penance." (See p. 27.) The contritionists replied that the disposition of which Trent speaks is remote. The attritionists on occasion called the contritionists "Jansenists." The contritionists in turn called the attritionists "laxists." When the controversy waxed warm and became the occasion of scandal, the Holy Office, at the direction of Pope Alexander VII, put an end to all name-calling by warning both parties not to brand the others' opinion with any theological note or censure. (*Decree of the Holy Office*, May 5, 1667; D1146) The decree, however, does admit that the position of the attritionists "appears to be more common among scholastics."

Today there is a tendency among attritionists to broaden the concept of attrition from the motive of fear. This fear must be understood as awe (*timor Domini*) in the presence of the Holy One who is all just, not craven fear in the presence of a despot. Trent had demanded that attrition from the motive of fear include the hope of divine pardon and that all contrition include confidence in the divine mercy. (See p. 27.) In this hope of pardon and confidence in God's mercy, attritionists find that initial love of God "as the source of all justice," of which Trent speaks in discussing the acts which are preparatory to justification. (D798) Attritionists, however, insist that this initial love is not one of benevolence or charity, but rather a love that is akin to the virtue of hope. God is loved not so much for his own goodness but for his goodness to me the sinner. Obviously, with God's grace this love of hope, or as some would put it, this love of concupiscence, can and perhaps ordinarily does yield to charity or love of God for his own sake. Struck with God's mercy toward the sinner, the sinner realizes that God is merciful to all sinners, that mercy is an attribute of God and hence lovable in itself. Our own view is that under the influence of the grace of the sacrament, a love which is at first self-regarding turns outward to God as the object of love.

Contritionists today have, for the most part, departed from their demands that the sinner must experience some initial love of benevolence or charity toward God before being absolved by the priest. Rather, they have returned to St. Thomas' teaching on contrition as the ultimate disposition for justification, in the sense that in and through the grace of absolution the penitent becomes contrite and thus disposed for the reception of grace and the forgiveness of sins. Thus grace has a twofold aspect. In the line of material cause, it disposes for justification; in the line of formal cause, it is the informing principle of justification. Whether or not contrition that results from the infusion of grace receives a new motivation, namely from charity, is not always made clear. To put the question another way, does the sinner who approaches absolution motivated by fear and hope experience a psychological change, whereby under the influence of the grace of the sacrament his sorrow is now motivated by charity? St. Thomas himself would seem to say yes, since he does not hold that attrition is changed into contrition by the presence of grace as an eliciting principle. (Cf. *Suppl.*, q.1, a.3.) Instead the attrite person becomes contrite through the grace of the sacrament, a view which suggests that the attrite person makes a new act of sorrow from a higher motive. As already noted above, we believe that ordinarily speaking the sinner, under the influence of the grace of the sacrament, does transform his motives for detesting sin, but we would not care to assert that a psychological transformation must have taken place in him.

## THE EFFECTS OF PENANCE

Theologians distinguish three elements in the sacraments: (1) the sacramental rite only (*sacramentum tantum*); (2) the reality and the inward sacrament, or symbolic reality (*res et sacramentum*); (3) the ultimate effect or reality only (*res tantum*). According to the Council of Trent, the sacramental rite is made up of the acts of the penitent, contrition, confession, and satisfaction, and the absolution of the priest. According to the same Council, the reality (*res*) or effect of the sacrament is reconciliation with God and, in some cases, peace and serenity of conscience along with an overwhelming consolation of spirit. (See p. 26.) Trent did not consider the second or intermediate element in the sacrament of penance, namely, the symbolic reality (*res et sacramentum*). However, it is this aspect of the sacrament of penance which is receiving most attention from theologians today. And it is in the light of their contributions that we can understand better the sacramental grace of penance, the grace which is distinctive of the sacrament of penance.

### *Symbolic Reality*

The symbolic reality is at once a reality (*res*) and a sacrament or sign (*sacramentum*) of a new relationship with Christ and his Church. Thus, in the sacrament of baptism the immediate effect (*res*) is the *baptismal character*, a spiritual reality which incorporates the baptized into the mystical body of Christ which is the Church. This "character" denotes in figure a stamp or impress whereby the Spirit achieves in the soul a likeness to Jesus Christ. The baptismal character is a sign of the

Christian's configuration or likeness to Christ as priest (*signum configurativum*), as well as a sign (*consecratorium*) of the Christian's consecration to the divine Three in whose name he has been baptized. Finally, the character disposes the soul for sanctifying grace and those other gifts and adornments which enable the baptized to live the life of a Christian and to take an active part in the priestly worship of the Church. Thus the immediate effect of the sacrament of baptism is not sanctifying grace itself, since a person can be baptized validly and receive the character without receiving grace. The immediate effect is the sacramental character which disposes the soul for grace provided no obstacle is placed in the way (*obex gratiae*.) Accordingly, theologians speak of the character as the dispositive sign of grace (*signum dispositivum*).

In the sacrament of penance no character is imprinted on the soul, nor, according to most theologians can the sacrament of penance be received validly without at the same time conferring grace. Yet a growing number of theologians hold that penance, like baptism, produces an effect which is prior (in nature, not in time) to the grace of divine forgiveness. Theologians, writing in the tradition of St. Thomas, find the symbolic reality of penance in that interior penance or contrition which is the ultimate disposition for the grace of divine pardon. Other theologians, including the present writer, find the symbolic reality in peace and reconciliation with the Church, a spiritual bond which disposes the soul for the life of grace which flows through the Church, Christ's mystical body. Just as the immediate effect of baptism is incorporation into the Church, so too the immediate effect of the sacrament of penance is reconciliation with the Church.

The advantage of this view is that it takes into account the social or ecclesial character of the sacrament of penance, which other theories fail to do sufficiently. Salvation ordinarily comes to the sinner in and through the Church. Through baptism he is incorporated into the Church, the domain of salvation, in which the Holy Spirit of Christ vitalizes those who are members of the Church. When this life of grace is lost through sin, the sinner is alienated not only from God but also from the Church. Although still a member of the Church, he is no longer a living member; he is no longer privileged to receive the eucharist, the sacrament of Christian unity. To this extent, even today, the serious sinner is in a true sense excommunicated, cut off from full communion with the Church. To be reconciled to God he must first be reconciled to the Church. So true is this that even when the sinner's sorrow is prompted by perfect love of God (perfect contrition) he must have the intention, explicit or implicit, of submitting his sins to the judgment of the Church.

Salvation, then, is not a wholly personal matter between God and the individual. In the case of baptism it involves entrance into the Church, in which and through which the sinner receives the grace of forgiveness. In the case of penance it involves reconciliation with the Church, in which and through which the sinner is reconciled to God. This, we believe, is the significance of Christ's words when he entrusted to his Church the power of forgiving sins. Speaking to the apostles and their successors as representatives of his Church, he says in effect: "Whose sins you forgive God will forgive; whose sins you retain, God will retain." Peace and reconciliation with the Church, to use a phrase frequently employed by the Fathers of the Church, is the efficacious sign or sacrament of divine forgiveness. As St. Augustine tersely expresses it, "The peace of the Church forgives sins, and separation from the Church's peace retains sins." (*On Baptism,* 3,18,23)

Reconciliation with the Church is then a reality (*res*) insofar as it establishes a new bond with the Church, and a sign (*sacramentum*) insofar as it disposes the soul for divine forgiveness. Continuing the parallel with the sacrament of baptism, we may ask the sense in which the penitent is configured or likened to Christ in the sacrament of penance. Recalling that the early Church frequently regarded the bishop as the vicar of God, and the fact that the bishop was the ordinary minister of reconciliation, we may say that the penitent in submitting to the bishop's judgment on sin is likened to Christ on Calvary submitting to the judgment of God the Father on sin. It is this submissiveness or readiness on the part of the sinner to atone for his sin that likens him to Christ who atoned vicariously for the sins of mankind.

In baptism the Christian in virtue of the sacramental character is likened to Christ as priest and is privileged to participate in the public worship of the Church. In the sacrament of penance the penitent is likened to Christ in his expiatory suffering. True, all the faithful have the obligation "to fill up what is wanting to the sufferings of Christ . . . for his body which is the Church." (Col 1,24) Since, however, the reconciled penitent differs from one who has never severed the bond of charity which unites the members of Christ's mystical body, it is understandable why the penitent is deputed in a special way to atone for the injury which he has done to the body of Christ, which is the Church. And it is precisely in submitting to the penances imposed by the Church through her priests that we are, as the Council of Trent asserts, "made like to Christ Jesus who satisfied for our sins." (See p. 29.)

## *Sacramental Grace of Penance*

Few authors treat *ex professo* the specific grace which distinguishes the sacrament of penance from the other sacraments. Like all the sacraments, the sacrament of penance confers the life of grace on the soul or increases it. However, in the case of serious sinners the grace given is a grace that is restored, the life given is a life that was lost. There is then a special modality to sanctifying grace that is conferred in the sacrament of penance. In baptism we receive the grace of regeneration and adoption as sons of God. In penance we receive the grace of reconciliation, the grace given to the prodigal son who has returned and who has been received again by the Father. Associated with this grace of reconciliation, which is the principal effect of the sacrament of penance, there is infused into the soul the special virtue of penance, a virtue which moves the sinner to make reparation for his sins, a virtue which is not infused at the time of baptism—except in the case of adults—since the virtue of penance supposes personal sins. However, if the virtue of penance is to become operative in works of penance, the penitent needs a special actual grace, a grace which will always be available since the reconciled sinner will always remain a penitent.

## *Reviviscence of Merits*

When a person sins mortally the good works which he performed in the state of grace cease to be of value. His store of merits is lost, but not irrevocably. According to the more common teaching of theologians today, these good works which become dead through sin (*opera mortificata*) are quickened or revive (*reviviscunt*) when the sinner returns to the state of grace. This view is supported by the teaching of Pius XI in his indulgence grant for the jubilee year 1925. Those who fulfill the conditions set down in the bull, "recover and receive in their entirety (*ex integro*) the fullness of those merits and gifts which they lost by sinning." (*Infinita Dei misericordia,* 29 May, 1924; D2193)

## *Value of Confessions of Devotion*

Since the principal effect of penance is reconciliation with God, it is understandable why, in the early Church, only those guilty of serious sins confessed to a priest. In the course of time, however, the practice of devotional confession—confession of venial sins or of sins already forgiven—was introduced. (See p. 18.) True, venial sins do not destroy the bond of charity which unites us to God and to his Church. Hence there can be no question of reconciliation either to God or to the Church in the strict sense of the term. And yet venial sins diminish the fervor of charity which should characterize the relation between God and the Christian. Again venial sins are an offense against the whole mystical body of Christ, of which the sinner is a member; for it is the Church's mission to be a witness, by the extraordinary sanctity of her members, to the truth of her claims as the Church of Christ. (Cf. *Vatican Council,* D1794.) If it be true, as many theologians teach, that the efficacy and value of the Mass is measured by the devotion and holiness of the Church which offers in sign Christ's sacrifice of Calvary, then it is understandable how even venial sins affect the Church's mission, which is not only to teach but to sanctify the world. Because of this social or ecclesial dimension of all sins, it is proper to confess even venial sins to the priest who is the representative of God and of the Church.

Such confessions of devotion also benefit and enrich the individual sinner. In recommending frequent confession in his encyclical on the mystical body, Pius XII lists some of the many benefits which result from the confession of venial sins: "By it genuine self knowledge is increased, Christian humility grows, evil habits are uprooted, spiritual neglect and tepidity are resisted, the conscience is purified, the will strengthened, a salutary control of one's affections gained, and in virtue of the sacrament itself grace is increased." (*Mystici Corporis,* n. 103, *AAS,* 35 [1943], 235)

A SUPPLEMENT

# INDULGENCES

An indulgence is the remission or, better, the payment from the Church's "treasury," of the temporal punishment due to sin after the guilt of sin has been forgiven. (Cf. *CIC,* Can. 911.) In this restricted sense, an indulgence grant is not met with until the eleventh century, when the practice was introduced of absolving penitents before the fulfillment of their penance. (See p. 19.) And yet, the principle underlying the practice of indulgences is as old as the Church herself. It is the principle of vicarious satisfaction, a principle which in turn is based on the doctrine of the communion of saints and the solidarity of all Christians in the one mystical body of Christ which is the Church. (Cf. 1 Cor 12,13.24–28; 2 Cor 1,11; Col 1,24.) Thus St. Paul rejoices in the sufferings which he bears for the Christians at Colossae, adding, "and what is wanting of the sufferings of Christ I fill up in my flesh for his body, which is the Church." (Col 1,24)

In the early Church, the principle of solidarity was given graphic expression in the discipline of the public penance, in which clergy and people associated themselves with the sinner in gaining complete pardon for an ailing member of Christ's body. Of particular efficacy were the intercessions of the martyrs who believed that their own sufferings could be of value to those who were less heroic in the persecutions.

When the discipline of public penance yielded to a private discipline, the sinner was not left to his own resources in expiating his sins. Through the use of an absolution grant, which was given either by the confessor immediately after sacramental reconciliation or by episcopal and papal letters, the sinner was assured of the special intercession of the Church on earth and in heaven for the sinner's complete pardon from every bond. Although scholars today do not see in these absolution grants instances of indulgences in the strict sense, the absolution grant did prepare the way for the more specific indulgence grant which remitted in whole or in part the penance assigned by the confessor. The earliest of such grants appears to have been the remission of one or two days of fasting during the period of Lent, for those who contributed to the support of the monastery church of San Pedro de Portella. (A.D. 1035; Cf. *Sources of Christian Theology,* 2, 330f) Similar partial indulgence grants were made in favor of other churches and religious establishments.

The earliest example of what appears to be a plenary indulgence was the Crusade Indulgence of Urban II (1095). Thus, "Whoever from devotion alone, and not for the purpose of gaining honors and wealth, shall set forth for the liberation of the Church of God at Jerusalem, that journey will be reckoned in place of all penance." (Council of Clermont, *Mansi,* 20, 815, Can. 11) Thus, penitents who had confessed—and Pope Urban insists on contrition and confession—were released from all penance imposed by their confessor on condition that they join the crusade. In the course of time the crusade indulgence was extended to all who contributed generously to the support of the crusade.

The theology of indulgences lagged more than a century behind the practice. The problem was to explain the efficacy of the indulgence grant in terms of the total redemptive mystery. Some were inclined to make the indulgence dependent upon the fervor and devotion of the one receiving it, or on the difficulty of the condition set down to gain it. Returning to the principle of vicarious satisfaction, St. Thomas stressed the idea, already advanced by Hugh of St. Cher (c. 1230), that the treasury of good works stored up by the whole mystical body, Christ and his members, is the source of the indulgence grant. Since these works of satisfaction are the common property of the Church, their distribution by way of indulgence grants should be made in accordance with the judgment of the one who presides over the community. (Cf. *S.Th., Suppl.,* 25,1.)

This idea of a common treasury as the source of the indulgence grant "to those who are truly penitent and have confessed" was confirmed by Clement VI in the Jubilee Bull of 1343. (Cf. D550–552.) A little more than a century later, Sixtus IV allowed indulgences to be applied to the souls in purgatory by way of prayer of petition (*per modum suffragii*). Such was the Church's official teaching on indulgences on the eve of the Protestant reformation. However, the abuses surrounding the practice of granting indulgences were real, and the exaggerated claims made at times by those who "trafficked" in indulgences tended to obscure the Church's teaching.

Yet the pre-Reformation picture is not entirely black. Not all the money collected on the occasion of an indulgence grant went to the purpose for which the indulgence was preached, but much of it did, as is evidenced by the number of monuments which remain. Cathedrals, monasteries, universities, schools, and hospitals were either built or kept in repair. In fact many of the social gains which we associate with European civilization are the direct or indirect result of indulgences. (Cf. N. Paulus, *Indulgences as a Social Factor.*) These are but the concomitant, of course, of the spiritual results of the indulgence grant, which are its primary effect. The preaching of an indulgence was the occasion of a great spiritual revival. Great preachers were invited to instruct the people, exhorting them to repent and to confess, the stipulated conditions for gaining the indulgence. Thus, a contemporary chronicler writes of the indulgence grant in favor of the cathedral of Speyer (1451), "there was such a great journeying to Speyer that often a hundred priests with their stoles sat hearing confessions." (Paulus, *op. cit.*, p. 24) Facts such as these belie the charge that an indulgence was either a license to sin or a substitute for the sacrament of penance.

At the Council of Trent, the right of the Church to grant indulgences was reaffirmed (D989). However, the fathers of the Council frankly admitted the abuses surrounding the practice and enacted disciplinary measures to correct them. In the year 1567, five years after Trent's disciplinary decrees, St. Pius V struck at the root of the abuses by abrogating "every indulgence . . . for which a helping hand must be offered, and which contains in any way whatsoever permission to make collections." (*Bullarium Romanum,* 7,535) This drastic step meant a serious loss of revenue to numerous churches, monasteries, hospitals and other charitable foundations. Because of it, however, instances of indulgence "traffic" are today nonexistent.

CHAPTER TWO

# THE SACRAMENT OF EXTREME UNCTION

## THE MINISTRY OF HEALING IN THE NEW TESTAMENT

In discussing the sacrament of penance we regarded the priestly ministry of reconciling sinners as the sacramental counterpart and continuation of Christ's ministry of forgiveness. In discussing the sacrament of extreme unction we may consider the priestly ministry of anointing the sick as the sacramental counterpart of Christ's ministry of healing. True, Christ's ministry of healing is continued more strikingly in the lives of Christian saints and miracle workers, but it is difficult to read the New Testament and the early formulas for blessing oil of the sick without coming to the conclusion that, over and above the more personal and charismatic gift of healing, there is present in Christ's Church a sacramental power which is attached to the rite of anointing the sick.

### *The Apostolic Ministry of Healing*

Christ's ministry of healing is summed up by Matthew: "And Jesus was going about all the towns and villages . . . curing every kind of disease and infirmity." (Mt 9,35) A few verses later, Christ's ministry of healing is entrusted to the apostles: "Then having summoned his twelve disciples, he gave them power over unclean spirits, to cast them out, and to cure every kind of disease and infirmity." (Mt 10,1) The parallel passages of Luke (9,1) and Mark (6,7.13) say the same. Mark, however, adds the significant detail that the cure of the sick was accompanied by an anointing with oil: "And going forth, they preached that men should repent, and they cast out many devils, and anointed with oil many sick people and healed them." (Mk 6,13)

It would not be proper to speak of the apostolic ministry of healing as a sacramental ministry in the strict sense of the word. The strict sacramental ministry of the apostles will begin at Pentecost and, except for baptism, be exercised only toward Christians. And yet we should see in this early rite of anointing with oil the real origins of the sacrament of unction. The power which the apostles received from Christ to assist those who are sick in body, in mind, and in spirit is the same power which Christ will entrust to his priests in the sacrament of order.

### *The Priestly Rite of Healing*

In its external details, the rite of anointing the sick described by the apostle James is basically the same as that administered by priests today:

> Is anyone among you sick? Let him bring in the presbyters of the Church, and let them pray over him, anointing him with oil in the name of the Lord. And the prayer of faith will save the sick man, and the Lord will raise him up, and if he be in sins, they shall be forgiven him. Confess, therefore, your sins to one another, and pray for one another, that you may be saved. For the unceasing prayer of a just man is of great avail. (Jas 5,14–16)

The recipient of the rite is one who is seriously sick, one who must summon the presbyters who will pray over him. The ministers of the rite are presbyters, a term which literally means elders, but one which the New Testament applies to the rulers of the local churches who were ordained to their office by the apostles or their coadjutors. (Cf. Ac 11,30; 14,23; 15,2; I Tim 5,17–19; Ti 1,5.) The rite itself is one of anointing with oil and prayer. The efficacy of the rite is ascribed to the Lord, in whose name the sick person has been anointed. The accompanying prayer of faith may mean a prayer inspired by the faith, or prayer said in faith and confidence. The words *save* and *raise up* have spiritual and psychological overtones, but it would seem that the specific purpose of the rite is the complete cure of the sick person. A conditioned effect of the rite is the forgiveness of sins, if the anointed one is burdened with them. The words "confess, therefore, your sins to one another" probably refer to a public acknowledgment of sinfulness on the part of the bystanders, an acknowledgment which would normally precede prayer, particularly prayer of petition. The last verse emphasizes the efficacy of prayer and suggests the need of confidence on the part of the ministers or those attending the sick person, a point that shall be stressed by the *Catechism of the Council of Trent*. (See p. 51.)

## EARLY EVIDENCE FOR RITE OF ANOINTING THE SICK

Apart from the exhortation of St. James there is little direct evidence for a priestly rite of anointing the sick before the year 400. Various reasons are assigned for this comparative silence. Unlike the rites of initiation, baptism, confirmation, and the eucharist and the rite of penance, the rite of anointing the sick was administered privately and hence attracted little attention and occasioned less explanation. Again, as a private rite performed by presbyters rather than by bishops who were the ordinary ministers of the other sacraments, marriage excepted, the rite of anointing the sick seems to have received no set prayers in the early liturgical books which have come down to us. These same works, however, contain formulas for blessing oil of the sick, a blessing or consecration usually reserved to the bishop. Finally, the earliest extant commentaries on the gospel according to Mark, in which a reference to the use of oil is made, is fifth century, while the earliest extant commentary on the epistle of James, in which the sacrament is recommended to the sick, is eighth century. And it is through the commentaries of the Fathers of the Church that we learn much of the Church's early teaching and practice.

### *Early Formulas for Blessing Oil of the Sick*

In the *Apostolic Tradition* of St. Hippolytus (c. 215) we have perhaps the earliest formula which clearly applies to oil of the sick. The oil is offered by the faithful and it is blessed by the bishop at the close of the canon of the Mass, a position still retained in the Roman rite for consecrating oil of the sick on Holy Thursday. The prayer asks that God may grant that the oil "may give strength to all that taste of it and health to all that use it." (5,2) A more detailed formula for blessing oil of the sick is found in the *Prayer Book (Euchologion)* of St. Serapion, compiled in Egypt in the middle of the fourth century. The prayer asks that God send down a curative power upon the oil so that "it may become a means of removing 'every disease and every sickness'"—a reference to Christ's ministry of healing and that of the Twelve—

> of warding off every demon, of putting to flight every unclean spirit, of keeping at a distance every evil spirit, of banishing all fever, all chill, and all weariness; a means of grace and goodness and the remission of sins; a medicament of life and salvation, unto health and soundness of soul and body and spirit, unto perfect well-being. (29)

The eighth century Gelasian rite for blessing oil of the sick invokes God to send the Holy Spirit upon the oil so that "Thy blessing may be to all who anoint, taste and touch a protection for body, soul and spirit, for dispelling all sufferings, all sickness, all illness of mind and body." (*Gelasian Sacramentary,* 1,40) The present *Roman Pontifical* has the same blessing as the *Gelasian Sacramentary* except for the phrase "to all who anoint, taste and touch." This has been changed to read: "to all who are anointed by this ointment of heavenly medicine."

These early formulas for blessing oil of the sick are important for the light that they throw on the purpose of the sacrament of unction. That purpose is best summed up in Serapion's expression "perfect well-being," that is, health and soundness of soul and body and spirit. Obviously, health of soul is more important than health of body, but the cure envisioned by the formulas is physical as well as spiritual, an effect which is proper to the sacrament of unction.

### *Practice of Anointing the Sick*

Early in the third century Tertullian criticized heretical women who had assumed functions which belong only to those properly ordained. Among these functions was the "promise to cure," a suggestion that the ministry of healing the sick belonged to the clergy. (*On the Prescription of Heretics,* 41) A few decades later, Origen cites the text from St. James in the context of confession to a priest of the Lord (*On Leviticus,* Homily 2), but it is not clear whether Origen has in mind the sacrament of penance alone or the combined rites of penance and unction in the case of sickbed penitents. With Innocent I (401–417) the practice of the Church becomes clear. There are two uses of oil of the sick which has been blessed by the bishop. The first is that of self-anointing or anointing by a layman; the second is that of anointing by a presbyter or bishop. This second type of anointing is called by Innocent "a kind of sacrament" and, as such, is not to be given to penitents, since they are denied the other sacraments, namely, reconciliation and the eucharist. (Cf. *Letter* 25, 8.)

Innocent's teaching is valuable for equating the rite of anointing the sick with the other sacraments. His teaching, however, raises the problem of the recipient of the rite. Today, unction can be given only to those in danger of death. In denying unction to penitents Innocent implies that the practice was not to anoint those who were dying but those who were sick, and yet not so seriously as to qualify for reconciliation and viaticum. We will suggest later that danger of death is a condition later introduced by the Western Church for disciplinary reasons, and that it was not an essential condition in the early Church.

In the early Middle Ages the custom of lay anointing was not only practiced but encouraged by such great bishops as Caesarius of Arles (d. 543) and Eligius of Noyon (d. 659). Both bishops exhort Christians to put their trust, in time of sickness, in the eucharist and in the oil of the sick, rather than to rely on the incantations of sorcerers, another indication that the purpose of anointing was to effect a cure and not to prepare the sick person for death. It would seem that oil of the sick, even when self-applied or when administered by one of the family, was regarded as having the same sacramental efficacy as the eucharist when self-administered. However, the memory of a more solemn anointing by presbyters was kept alive by repeated reference, even in the exhortations of Caesarius and Eligius, to the text of James, which exhorts the faithful who are sick to call in the presbyters of the Church.

In England, Bede the Venerable (d. 735), whose commentary on the Epistle of St. James is the first to come down to us, admits the legitimacy of lay anointing, but refers to the rite described by Mark and by James as the "custom of the Church." (*On the Epistle of James,* 5) It is of interest to note that the custom, according to Bede, embraced "possessed persons or any others who are sick." (*On the Gospel of Mark,* 6) On the continent, just prior to the Carolingian reform, it would appear that priests were less zealous in their duty of visiting the sick. In any event the reform movement was initiated by Alcuin of York at the close of the eighth century and in the succeeding century a number of local councils were held in the Frankish kingdom to legislate reform measures. Typical of these measures was the insistence that bishops bless oil of the sick on Holy Thursday and that sick persons be not deprived through the presbyter's carelessness of confession, reconciliation, and the anointing with consecrated oil. (Cf. II Council of Aachen, A.D. 836, *Mansi,* 14, 104.) The Council of Mainz (847) places the anointing of the sick in the context of confession, reconciliation, and viatioum, with viaticum the last sacrament in what we may now refer to as the "last rites of the dying." Prior to this time, however, there is no evidence that the anointing was reserved only for those who were in danger of death.

## *An Early Rite of Anointing the Sick*

Although a formula for blessing oil of the sick is found in the third century *Apostolic Tradition* of Hippolytus (see p. 45), the earliest description of the actual anointing is perhaps the ninth century Carolingian rite which is appended to Alcuin's *Order for Visiting the Sick* in the *Gregorian Sacramentary* as found in Migne. After a series of prayers in which the text of James is incorporated and which asks that the sick person be restored to "full health, both inwardly and outwardly," and that "he may be strengthened to take up again his former duties," the sick person is anointed. The anointing is similar to that of baptism, on the back of the neck and on the throat, between the shoulders and on the breast or "let him anoint further the place where the pain is more pronounced." The first part of the prayer or formula for unction is derived from the rite of exorcising catechumens; the second part is more specific: "And through this ointment of consecrated oil and our prayer, cured and warmed by the Holy Spirit, may you merit to receive your former and even better health." A closing rubric, which is probably not part of the original rite, states that many priests anoint the sick also on the five senses saying: "In the name of the Father, and of the Son, and of the Holy Spirit." In the course of time these five senses will be anointed as the organs or instruments of sin, and the formula of the sacrament will pray that the Lord will forgive the sins committed through these senses, as in the Roman rite today. Apart from this development, the prayers of the *Gregorian Sacramentary* asking for the sick person's restoration to health are still found in the present Roman rite. In neither rite is there any suggestion that the purpose of unction is to prepare the sick person for death. This is a development of the scholastic period, which we shall now consider.

## SCHOLASTIC SPECULATION

By the middle of the twelfth century, the practice of postponing the anointing until the sick person was near death had become so widespread that theologians of the period began to refer to the anointing of the sick as the sacrament of the departing (*exeuntium*), a sacrament to be administered *in extremis,* or as Peter Lombard called it, the sacrament of extreme unction. By the close of the century, the custom was gradually introduced of inverting the order of unction and viaticum, so that unction became in fact the last sacrament to be administered, supplanting viaticum as the Church's parting gift—a climactic position which unction retained up until recent years when the original order of penance, unction, and viaticum was restored in the new ritual for the United States. (See *Collectio Rituum,* Bruce, 1954.)

Faced with what was in fact the last sacrament or sacrament of the dying, it is understandable that the great scholastic doctors of the thirteenth century should agree that the purpose of the rite of anointing is to prepare the soul for death and for immediate entrance into heaven. They also agreed that the recipient of the sacrament should be one who is actually departing this life. Their main point of disagreement concerned the principal effect of the sacrament. Bonaventure and Scotus of the Franciscan school argued that the principal obstacle to a life of glory is the presence in the soul of venial sins. Accordingly, the principal effect of the sacrament of the departing should be the final remission of venial sins. To make sure that this remission would be final, Scotus demanded that unction be given only to one who is so close to death as to be incapable of further sin. (*4 Sent.* 23,2.1) Albert the Great and Thomas Aquinas of the Dominican school argued that the remission of the guilt of sin, whether mortal or venial, was the proper effect of the sacrament of penance and not of unction. However, since all agreed that the effect of unction was the remission of sin in some sense of the term, Albert and Thomas held that the principal effect of unction was the removal of the consequences (*reliquiae*) of sin, namely that general weakness or lassitude of soul which is the aftermath of sin, both original and personal, and which renders a soul less ready to live a life of glory. To cite Thomas directly: "Hence it must be said that the principal effect of this sacrament is the remission of sins with respect to the remnants of sin, and by way of consequence also with respect to guilt, if it should find it present." (*Supplement*, 30,1) In the *Summa Contra Gentes* Thomas also holds that through unction which perfects penance "the person is freed of the debt of temporal punishment, so that, when the soul departs from the body, nothing remains to prevent its entrance into glory. (*S.C.G.*, 4,73)

## THE REFORMATION AND TRENT

### *Teaching of Reformers*

Protestants of all denominations deny that extreme unction is a sacrament instituted by Christ. The reasons for their denial are basically what they were at the time of the Protestant reformation. According to Martin Luther, the practice of anointing was instituted by the Church and hence is to be numbered among those "sacraments" of human, ecclesiastical institution, such as the blessing of salt or the sprinkling with holy water. Questioning the authenticity of the epistle of James, Luther insists that it is faith and confidence on the part of the recipient and not the anointing and prayer of the priest which cures the sick person and forgives his sins. (*Babylonian Captivity*, 7) Luther does score one point when he criticizes the exaggerated practice of anointing only when the person is at the brink of death, a criticism which will be made by the *Catechism of the Council of Trent*.

John Calvin not only denies the sacramentality of the rite of anointing the sick but goes beyond Luther in criticizing its continued use as "mere hypocritical stage-play." The gift of healing, he maintained, was given to the apostles and it disappeared with the other miraculous powers which the Lord was pleased to give to the early Church. The forgiveness of sins of which James speaks is not to be attributed to the anointing with oil but to the prayers of believers. (*Institutes of the Christian Religion*, 4,18,21)

With the exception of the Anglo-Catholics, Anglicans and Episcopalians generally do not anoint the sick on their visitation to them. The Anglican *Thirty-Nine Articles* (1563) recognize only two sacraments, baptism and the Lord's supper. The other five were not instituted by Christ. The rite of anointing the sick does not appear in the *Anglican Prayer Book* after the first edition of 1549. However, the *American Prayer Book* adapted for Episcopalians has an optional rite of anointing or an imposition of the hand.

## *Teaching of Trent*

In its Canons on extreme unction the fathers at Trent (Session XIV, 1551) anathematize those who maintain: (1) that extreme unction is not a sacrament instituted by Christ and promulgated by the apostle James; (2) that the rite does not confer grace, or remit sin, or relieve the sick, but that it has now ceased to be operative as though in times past it was only a grace of healing; (3) that the rite and usage of the Church are contrary to the statement of James, and are therefore to be changed, and can be contemned by Christians without sin; (4) that the presbyters of the Church mentioned by James are not priests ordained by a bishop, but elders of the community, and that, on this account the proper minister of extreme unction is not the priest alone. (Cf. D926–929.)

The doctrinal chapters of Trent are more positive and instructive. Here, the teaching is developed with special reference to the dying Christian, since it is especially at the time of death that our adversary, Satan, "strains more relentlessly all the cunning of his resources to destroy us completely, and if possible, to disturb our confidence in the divine mercy." (D907) After discoursing on the institution of the sacrament by Christ and its promulgation by James, Trent teaches that the matter of the sacrament is oil blessed by the bishop and the form the words: "Per istam unctionem. . . ." [In an emergency the short formula, which is found in the ritual, may be given: "By this holy anointing may the Lord pardon you whatsoever you have done amiss. Amen."]

The reality (*res*) and effect of the rite is "the grace of the Holy Spirit, whose anointing wipes away sins, provided there are still some to be expiated, as well as the remnants of sin (*peccati reliquias*); it also comforts and strengthens the soul of the sick person, by arousing in him great confidence in the divine mercy. Encouraged thereby, the sick person bears more easily the difficulties and trials of his illness, and resists more readily the temptations of the demon who *lies in wait for the heel* (Gn 3,15), and, where it is expedient for the health of the soul, he receives, at times, health of body." (D909)

The proper ministers of the sacrament are the presbyters of the Church, a term which refers to bishops or priests duly ordained. An early draft of the decree on extreme unction proposed that the sacrament be given "only to those who are in their final struggle, who have come to grips with death and who are about to go forth to the Lord." Providentially, the final draft reads that this anointing "is to be used for the sick, but especially for those who are so dangerously ill as to appear at the point of departing this life." (D910)

### *Catechism of the Council of Trent*

Written on the advice of the fathers of Trent, the *Catechismus Romanus* (1566) prescribes that only when the danger of death is present may extreme unction be administered. It is considered in this book "a very grievous sin to defer holy unction until, all hope of recovery being lost, life begins to ebb, and the sick person is fast verging into a state of insensibility." Pastors, therefore, should be careful to administer the sacrament when it can be aided in its effectiveness by the piety and devotion of the sick person.

In speaking of the recovery of health as an effect of the anointing, the catechism offers two reasons to explain why this effect obtains less frequently in our days: (1) this is not owing to any defect in the sacrament but rather to the weaker faith of a great part of those who are anointed with the sacred oil or by whom it is administered; (2) the Church stands less in need of miracles, now that she is firmly rooted, than she did in her infancy. (*Catechism of the Council of Trent,* Part II, "The Sacraments")

## RECENT CONTRIBUTIONS

Much has been written on the sacrament of extreme unction in recent years. In general there is a tendency among modern authors to regard unction as a sacrament of the sick rather than as a sacrament of the dying. This is not to deny that those who are dying are also sick. However it is felt, generally, that long before death is imminent or even proximate the sick person would profit by the many actual graces which are given to support him in his illness.

The Council of Trent in its decree on penance teaches that satisfaction can be made to God by patiently enduring the sufferings of this life; in its decree on unction it teaches that special graces are given to help us bear more easily the trials and difficulties of illness. (See pp. 29, 50.) In the light of this teaching we can more readily understand the sense in which one effect of the grace of unction is the remission of the temporal punishment due to sin. Not that unction remits the punishment directly; rather grace is given to bear those trials and sufferings by which the debt of punishment is paid. Again, we can understand how a prolonged illness rather than the recovery of health can be more expedient for the soul of the sick person, as Trent states. (See p. 50.) Sickness when supported by the grace of unction can purify the soul of those remnants of sin of which Trent speaks, as well as expiate the punishment due to sin, thus preparing the soul for immediate entrance into heaven. Again, if unction is administered in the early stages of serious sickness there is more likelihood that the curative powers of the sacrament will be operative, more likelihood that the sick person as well as the ministering priest will have great confidence in obtaining the effect for which the ritual prays: the restoration to "full health, both inwardly and outwardly, that having recovered with the help of Your mercy he (she) may once more have strength to take up his (her) former duties."

The main difficulty against anointing in the early stages of serious illness is the teaching of theologians, confirmed by the Code of Canon Law which states that "Extreme unction cannot be given except to one of the faithful who, after reaching the use of reason, on account of illness or old age, is in danger of death." (Can. 940) More recent theologians, however, tend to interpret the phrase "danger of death" quite liberally. Thus, danger of death need not be imminent nor even proximate; remote danger of death is sufficient, a danger which is present in most cases of serious illness. Again, danger of death need not be real or objective. It is enough that there be a prudent judgment that there is such danger. This more liberal view is confirmed by an apostolic letter of Pius XI: "For it is not necessary either for the validity or the lawfulness of the sacrament that death be feared as something proximate; rather, it is enough that there should be a prudent or probable judgment of danger." (*Explorata res,* Feb. 2, 1923; *AAS,* 15,105) Some theologians have even requested the Holy See to clarify the issue by substituting in the Code of Canon Law "serious illness" for "danger of death," a change that would emphasize unction as a sacrament of the sick rather than as a sacrament of the dying. This change in wording would authorize a pastoral preaching and instruction that would help to allay the fears of many of the faithful who are reluctant to receive a sacrament which in practice is regarded as a harbinger of death.

PART TWO

# THE SACRAMENTS OF VOCATION

All seven sacraments are part of the Church's public worship, and all seven consecrate the recipient to the Church's service. Again, the grace of all the sacraments is given in and through the Church, the mystical body of Christ. To this extent we may regard all the sacraments as social or ecclesial. There are, however, two sacraments which are pre-eminently social. They look more to the well-being of the whole Christian community than to the personal sanctification and enrichment of the individual. These are the sacraments of order and marriage. A priest is not ordained for himself but for the Church. A man and a woman are married not so much for their own personal fulfillment but for the family which is the Church in miniature. Bishops and priests are ordained to assure the spiritual growth and religious direction of the Christian community. Husbands and wives are married to assure the physical growth and continuity of the Church until the day of the Lord's coming. In this sense, order and marriage may be called vocational sacraments. They consecrate a state of life which is dedicated to the spiritual and physical growth of God's people on earth. Although the two states or vocations are by no means incompatible—the Eastern rites of the Church have a married lower clergy—there are, as we shall see, special reasons which recommend celibacy in those who have been called to govern and direct the larger family which is the Church of God.

CHAPTER THREE

# THE SACRAMENT OF ORDER

The Church, the mystical body of Christ, is an ordered society which has multiple sacred functions. Responsibility for these is distributed among various grades or orders, when it is a question of the role of the clergy in the life of the Church. From the point of view of jurisdiction or external government the sacred hierarchy is made up of the first or Roman bishop ("supreme pontiff") and the college of bishops. From the point of view of order or the sacred ministry the sacred hierarchy is made up of bishops, presbyters (priests), and ministers (deacons). According to the Council of Trent, this hierarchy of orders is of divine arrangement. Besides the three grades mentioned, the Eastern Church recognizes but two additional grades or orders, those of subdeacon and reader. Other grades, however, were introduced into the Western Church sometime in the third century and are recognized by the Western Church today. They are the grades of acolyte, exorcist, and porter. In the Eastern Church the subdiaconate is regarded as a minor order. Subdeacons are allowed to marry. In the Western Church the subdiaconate is listed among the major orders. Subdeacons are not only forbidden to marry but are also obliged to recite the divine office, the public prayer of the Church.

In the Eastern Church, the diaconate is often terminal. In the Western Church, all orders, both major and minor, are regarded as grades or steps leading up to the priesthood. They are at the service of the priesthood, and they have been instituted in order that the priest's ministry be exercised more worthily and with greater dignity. (Cf. Council of Trent, D958,962.) Since it is the Christian priesthood as verified in bishops and presbyters which is central to the sacrament of order, our study of order begins with the priesthood and the manner in which others are called upon or ordained to carry on Christ's priesthood. Our primary source is the New Testament.

## THE NEW TESTAMENT WITNESS

### *The Priesthood of Christ*

Jesus Christ is the only priest of the New Testament. He is the sole mediator between God and man. His mediatorship is both godward and manward, ascendant and descendant. As priest, he brings to God our petitions, our expressions of sorrow, our praise, our thanksgiving. All this he does as High Priest in the continued offering of the Mass, in which sacramental making-present of His one sacrifice he remains the principal priest. As priest, he brings to men God's truth, God's law, and God's life He is the truth, the way, and the life. He is prophet, king, and priest, three titles which express the fullness of his priesthood. Christ's priesthood is eternal. Unlike the priests of the Old Law, Christ can have no successors in the priesthood. Christian priests are not ordained to succeed Christ but to continue his priesthood, to give visible expression to his continuing priesthood, and to share in that priesthood.

In the eucharistic sacrifice and in the administration of the sacraments, it is Christ the unique priest who works through his chosen ministers. In the pastoral role of teaching, guiding, and ruling the Church it is Christ who is operative as the supreme shepherd of his flock. It is he who teaches, guides, and rules through his ordained pastors. "He who hears you, hears me; and he who rejects you, rejects me; and he who rejects me, rejects him who sent me." (Lk 10,16)

## *The Priesthood of the Apostles*

The apostles are never called priests in the New Testament. The term priest is applied to Christ in the epistle to the Hebrews; to the whole Christian people by the first epistle of St. Peter, which speaks of "a holy priesthood" (1 Pt 2,5) and again "a royal priesthood." (2,9) Yet no one can reasonably doubt that the priestly and pastoral office was entrusted to the apostles by Christ, the unique priest and shepherd. Early in Christ's public ministry, the Twelve were sent to preach repentance, to drive out devils, and to heal the sick. (Cf. Mt 10,1; Lk 9,1; Mk 6,7.) On the night of the resurrection they were given power to forgive sins. (Jn 20,21–23) On the night before he suffered they were consecrated priests in the strict meaning of the term, for on that night they were commissioned to do what Christ had done: to offer the eucharistic sacrifice in memory of him. (Cf. Lk 22,19; 1 Cor 11,24; Council of Trent, D938,949.) Although there is no indication in Acts that the apostles reserved to themselves the celebration of the Lord's supper, we may presume that, as head of the local churches founded by them, they or those appointed or ordained by them would preside over the eucharistic sacrifice. This presumption is verified by Clement of Rome (c. 96), by Ignatius of Antioch (c. 110), and by the whole Christian tradition. (See p. 62.)

Although the apostles were consecrated priests at the last supper, no rite or ceremony of ordination is recorded. Nor was there any need of a symbolic rite to express Christ's will to invest his apostles with priestly powers. The earliest accounts of a rite of investiture or ordination are found in Acts and in the pastoral epistles to Timothy. We shall consider them in order.

## *Ordination of Deacons*

The word deacon (*diákonos*) means a minister or servant. It is frequently used in the New Testament of one who serves at table.

However, the term is also used of one who ministers to the spiritual needs of others. Thus, Christ is called "the minister (*diákonos*) to the circumcised" (Rom 15,8); St. Paul refers to himself as "the minister (*diákonos*)" of the gospel. (Eph 3,7) However, Paul also uses the word *diákonos* to refer to a special grade in the hierarchy which is distinguished from the grade of bishop and/or presbyter. (Phil 1,1; cf. 1 Tim 3,8–13.) Although the noun *diákonos* is not used in referring to the seven who are ordained by an imposition of the hands in our present text (Ac 6,1–6), Christian tradition has early regarded their ordination as an ordination to the distinct grade of deacon. The text follows.

> Now in those days, as the number of the disciples was increasing, there arose a murmuring among the Hellenists against the Hebrews that their widows were being neglected in the daily ministration. So the Twelve called together the multitude of the disciples and said, "It is not desirable that we should forsake the word of God and serve at tables. Therefore, brethren, select from among you seven men of good reputation, full of the Spirit and of wisdom, that we may put them in charge of this work. But we will devote ourselves to prayer and to the ministry of the word." And the plan met the approval of the whole multitude, and they chose Stephen, a man full of faith and of the Holy Spirit, and Philip and Prochorus and Nicanor and Timon and Parmenas and Nicholas, a proselyte from Antioch. These they set before the apostles, and after they had prayed laid their hands upon them. (Ac 6,1–6)

The rite described here, prayer and an imposition of hands, is essentially the rite of ordination today. There is, however, one difficulty in seeing in the present rite a sacrament which confers grace. The office to which the deacon is ordained today is primarily spiritual; he is empowered to baptize solemnly, to sing or read the gospel, and to assist the bishop or priest at the eucharistic sacrifice. The seven deacons of Acts seem to be ordained to an office that is purely temporal: serving at tables. Yet the context suggests that their ministry was also spiritual. They are to be men filled with the Holy Spirit and wisdom. The table which they will serve will at times be that of the *agápē* which was held in the primitive Church in conjunction with the eucharist. Finally, two at least of the seven, Philip and Stephen, actually exercised a spiritual ministry. Immediately after his ordination, we read that Stephen, "full of grace and strength, worked great wonders and signs among the people," and that he preached Christ to the Jews and was martyred for his witness. (Cf. Ac 6,8–7,60.) Philip also preached the gospel in Samaria and baptized. (Cf. Ac 8,5.36–40.)

### *Ordination of Saul and Barnabas*

Although Paul testifies that he was chosen directly by Christ for the apostolate, it is not unlikely that he was ordained along with Barnabas for his special mission to the gentiles. The passage occurs in Ac 13,1ff.

> Now in the Church at Antioch there were prophets and teachers, among whom were Barnabas and Simon, called Niger, and Lucius of Cyrene, and Manahen the foster brother of Herod the tetrarch, and Saul. And as they were ministering to the Lord and fasting, the Holy Spirit said, "Set apart for me Saul and Barnabas unto the work to which I have called them." Then, having fasted and prayed and laid their hands upon them, they let them go.

### *Appointment of Presbyter-Bishops*

The terms presbyter and bishop (*epískopos*) are used interchangeably in Acts and in the epistles of St. Paul. The term *présbyter* (elder) seems to refer to the honor or dignity of the office, whereas bishop seems to refer to the presbyter's function of ruling the Church of God. In Ac 14,23, we read that Paul and Barnabas appointed presbyters in the various churches which they founded. Paul sends to Ephesus "for the presbyters of the Church" (Ac 20,17), and in a discourse to them he calls them bishops: "Take heed to yourselves and to the whole flock in which the Holy Spirit has placed you as bishops to rule (literally, to shepherd) the Church of God." (Ac 20,28) This pastoral office of presbyter-bishop is mentioned in the following words of 1 Pt: "Now I exhort the presbyters among you—I, your fellow presbyter . . . tend the flock of Christ which is among you, governing (*episkopoûntes*) not by constraint but willingly according to God." (1 Pt 5,1–3) Accordingly, presbyters are not simply elders in the sense of older members of the Christian community who hold a position of honor. They were appointed or ordained to their office and had a definite function as divinely established bishops to rule and shepherd the Church of God.

### *Ordination of Timothy*



Paul's account of the ordination of his fellow-worker Timothy is the classical reference, appealed to by the Council of Trent, for the sacramentality of the rite of order. (Cf. D959.) In 1 Tim 4,14, Paul exhorts Timothy: "Do not neglect the grace that is in you, granted to you by reason of prophecy with the laying on of hands of the presbyterate." In 2 Tim 1,6–8, Paul again reminds him of the grace of office which he received through the imposition of hands, but Paul now includes himself among the ordaining presbyters:

> For this reason I admonish you to stir up the grace of God which is in you by the laying on of my hands. For God has not given us the spirit of fear, but of power and of love and of prudence.

The Greek word for grace is *chárisma,* a generic term which means gift. In the present context the gift in question is the spirit "of power, and of love and of prudence," gifts which admittedly enrich and sanctify the recipient, but gifts which are designed principally to equip Timothy for his pastoral office. Whatever the nature and complexity of this charism it is a gift of God, yet conferred by Paul and the presbyters through an imposition of the hands. Paul does not mention a prayer accompanying the imposition of the hands, but earlier descriptions in Ac 6,1–6 and 13,3, together with early Christian practice, allow us to conclude that Timothy's ordination was ritually the same as sacramental ordinations today, an imposition of the hands and an accompanying prayer. Catholic tradition has seen in Timothy's ordination an elevation to the episcopate. He was, however, a missionary bishop, and it would seem a coadjutor or assistant of Paul, who apparently kept in his own hands the external government of the Churches he founded.

### *A Charismatic Ministry?*

Over and above the hierarchy made up of presbyter-bishops and deacons, Paul refers time and again to certain individuals who appear to have special functions in the Christian community. Moreover, they appear to have received special charismatic gifts for the fulfillment of their office. Thus, in Eph 4,7, we read: "But to each one of us grace was given according to the measure of Christ's bestowal." In this context Paul gathers together four classes of individuals who seem to have been appointed to a special ministry: "And he himself gave some men as apostles, and some as prophets, others again as evangelists, and others as pastors and teachers in order to perfect the saints for a work of ministry, for building up the body of Christ. . . ." (Eph 4,11.12)

Liberal Protestants, writing in the tradition of A. von Harnack, regard the men mentioned by Paul as making up a primitive ministry which antedated the institutional hierarchy of presbyter-bishops and deacons. More conservative Protestants distinguish between what might be called a hierarchy of occurrence and a hierarchy of institution, both equally primitive. The ministry of occurrence waits upon the inspiration or direct intervention of the Spirit; the ministry of institution awaits the imposition of hands by the clergy. Personally, we believe that the distinction between a charismatic ministry or ministry of occurrence and an institutional ministry of orders is overdrawn. The ministry of institution is conferred in a rite which gives a variety of gifts or charisms. There is no reason to believe that the special graces which are given apostles, evangelists, teachers, and pastors of whom Paul speaks, were given directly by God apart from an ordination rite. This does not mean that the Holy Spirit restricted his gifts to the members of the hierarchy, any more than he does so today. There were prophets and prophetesses among the laity as well as among the clergy, just as there are saints and mystics and catechists among the laity today.

## EARLY DEVELOPMENT OF ORDERS

### *A Sacrificial Priesthood*

Nowhere in Acts or in the epistles of St. Paul is the office of bishop or presbyter described as sacrificial or priestly in the strict meaning of the word. The first writer to suggest that the principal function of the apostles and their immediate successors was to offer sacrifice is Pope Clement I (c. 96). Of interest as well is Clement's description of the early hierarchy as made up of bishops and deacons, with no reference to a distinct grade of presbyter. The passage is worth citing at length, as a description of the manner in which the apostolic ministry was continued in the primitive Church.

> The Apostles preached to us the Gospel received from Jesus Christ, and Jesus Christ was God's Ambassador. . . . From land to land, accordingly, and from city to city they preached, and from among their earliest converts appointed men whom they had tested by the Spirit to act as bishops and deacons for the believers. . . . Our Apostles, too, were given to understand by our Lord Jesus Christ that the office of the bishop would give rise to intrigues. For this reason, equipped as they were with perfect foreknowledge, they appointed the men mentioned above, and afterwards laid down a rule once for all to this effect: when these men die, other approved men shall suc-

ceed to their sacred ministry (*leitourgían*). Consequently, we deem it an injustice to eject from the sacred ministry the persons who were appointed either by them, or later, with the consent of the whole Church, by other men in high repute and have ministered to the flock of Christ faultlessly, humbly, quietly and unselfishly, and have moreover, over a long period of time, earned the esteem of all. Indeed, it will be no small sin for us if we oust men who have irreproachably and piously offered the sacrifices (*tà dōra*) proper to the episcopate. (*Epistle to the Corinthians,* 42,44, tr. by J. Kleist, *ACW,* I; cited with permission of the Newman Press, Westminster, Md.)

The use of the word *leitourgía* to describe the ministry of the bishop indicates that his ministry was one of cult or worship, characterized by offering "the gifts of the Church." Kleist translates *tà dōra* as sacrifices, not without reason. A century later Hippolytus uses the same expression *tà dōra* to express the object of the bishop's sacrifice, "the bread and the cup," which the newly ordained bishop is to offer "making eucharist to You, because You have bidden us to stand before You and minister as priests to You." (*The Apostolic Tradition,* 4,11) From the time of Hippolytus the word priest will be applied to the bishop and then in time (fourth century) to the presbyter, who will gradually begin to take over many of the bishop's functions in the more populous churches of the East and the West.

### *The Monarchical Bishop*

The first writer to distinguish the bishop from the presbyter is St. Ignatius of Antioch (c. 110). It would seem that in the churches founded by St. John, the monarchical bishop was separated early from his fellow presbyters and assumed a position of prominence. Like Clement of Rome, Ignatius stresses the strictly sacrificial function of the bishop. The celebration of the eucharist is legitimate only when held under the bishop or by one appointed by him. (Cf. *To the Smyrnaeans,* 8.) A picture of the threefold hierarchy with the monarchical bishop as head of the Christian community is given in Ignatius' letter *To the Philippians*: "Take care, then, to partake of one eucharist, for one is the flesh of our Lord Jesus Christ, and one the cup to unite us with his blood, and one altar, just as there is one bishop, assisted by the presbytery and the deacons my fellow servants." (4)

### *Ordination Rites of Hippolytus*



The earliest detailed ordinal or bishop's book for the early liturgy is the *Apostolic Tradition* of Hippolytus, compiled from earlier sources about the year 215. The ordinal clearly distinguishes between ordination through an imposition of hands and simple appointment. Thus, bishops, presbyters, and deacons are ordained. Subdeacons, readers, and widows are appointed without imposition of hands. There is no reference to acolytes, exorcists, or porters. Later in the century these minor orders will be introduced into the Church of the West but not into the Church of the East. All this would indicate that the subdiaconate and the minor orders are not part of the sacrament of order but sacramentals.

ORDINATION OF BISHOPS The bishop is chosen by all the people, but he is ordained by an imposition of hands by his fellow bishops alone. The prayer for consecration stresses the pastoral and priestly office of the bishop. He is to forgive sins and minister to God as high priest. The power given to Jesus and bestowed on the apostles is invoked. In the prayer of consecration and in the liturgy which follows the strictly sacerdotal function of the bishop is stressed. (II, III)

ORDINATION OF THE PRESBYTER The presbyter is ordained by the imposition of the hands of the bishop accompanied by that of the presbyters. The grace invoked is the "spirit of grace and counsel, that he may share in the presbyterate and govern Your people in a pure heart." (VIII) Here, an allusion is made to the seventy presbyters or elders who shared in the spirit given to Moses to govern the people of God in the Desert. (Cf. Nm 11,16.)

ORDINATION OF THE DEACON The bishop alone lays hands on the candidate. The latter is reminded that he is not ordained for a priesthood as are the presbyters, but for the service of the bishops. The Holy Spirit of grace and earnestness and diligence is invoked upon the candidate, who is to minister (*diakónein*) to the Church and to bring up the gifts to be offered by the bishop or high priest, a reference to the deacon's function at the offertory of the Mass. (IX)

## EARLY HERESIES

### *Montanism*

The first to challenge the hierarchical constitution of the Church were the Montanists at the close of the second century. Their ablest spokesman was Tertullian after his defection from the Church. As a Catholic he had ridiculed the ordination of women in heretical sects and the heretical practice of allowing laymen to assume priestly functions.

(Cf. *On the Prescription of Heretics,* 41.) As a Montanist, however, he maintained that the distinction between clergy and laity was made by the Church, and that before God the layman was on a par with the bishop. Like the bishop, he should be a man but once married. In his attack on the right of a Catholic bishop to forgive serious sins, he shows his Montanist tendencies by claiming this right for the Church of the Spirit but denying it to the Church which is made up of bishops. (Cf. *On Modesty,* 21; see p. 20.)

### *Donatism*

The Donatists take their name from Donatus, schismatical bishop of Carthage (315), who denied the validity of sacraments administered by heretical and, ironically enough, by schismatical bishops. The Donatist position was condemned at the Council of Arles (314) and again at the Council of Nicaea (325), but the schism continued and found its ablest opponent in the person of St. Augustine, bishop of Hippo. From Augustine we have the basic principle in sacramental theology that neither orthodox faith nor holiness are required in the person of the minister of the sacraments, provided he has been validly ordained. From Augustine, too, we have the first explicit teaching on the sacramental character which renders the sacraments of baptism, confirmation, and order permanent and indelible sacraments. They can neither be effaced nor repeated. Comparing baptism and order, Augustine states that "each is a sacrament, and is given to a man by a kind of consecration: the one when he is baptized, the other when he is ordained. For this reason neither allows of repetition in the Church of God." (*Against Parmenian,* 2,13,38) Augustine concludes that even Donatist bishops are not to be reordained when they have abjured their errors and have returned to the Catholic Church.

## THE MIDDLE AGES

### *Revival of Heresies*

The thirteenth century was marked by a spirit of reform which found authentic expression in the great mendicant orders founded by St. Dominic and St. Francis of Assisi. Equally zealous for reform were the Waldensians or "poor men of Lyons," who regarded evangelical
 poverty as the highest norm of sanctity. They taught that only those who practiced it, whether laymen or clerics, were worthy to preach the

gospel and to administer the sacraments. The Waldensians were condemned by Pope Innocent III in 1208. (Cf. D423.) Two centuries later the principles of Peter Waldo, the founder of this sect, were revived by John Wycliffe, who had his own group of "poor preachers" sent out to reform the Church, and by John Hus. The Wycliffites and the Hussites were condemned at the Council of Constance in 1415. (Cf. D581ff.)

## *Scholastic Contributions*

By the middle of the twelfth century order or ordination was numbered among the seven sacraments of the Church and defined as such in the profession of faith drawn up for the Eastern emperor Palaeologus at the second Council of Lyons in 1274. (Cf. D465.) One of the principal contributions of the early scholastic doctors was to revive Augustine's teaching on the sacramental character and thus put an end to the practice of reordaining clerics who had been ordained by bishops guilty of simony and other vices. On other questions concerning the sacrament of order there was not the same unanimity. Speculation centered on: (1) the distinction between the bishop and the presbyter; (2) the sacramentality of the subdiaconate and the minor orders; (3) the unity of the sacrament of order.

The prevailing view was that of St. Thomas who held (1) that episcopacy as such is not a distinct order from that of priesthood and, it would seem, is not conferred in a strict sacramental rite (*Suppl.*, 40,5); (2) that priesthood and all six orders leading up to priesthood imprint a character and hence are part of the one sacrament of order (*Suppl.*, 35,2); (3) that the orders leading up to priesthood are parts of the one sacrament of order which is conferred fully in the priesthood and partially or by way of participation in the other sacramental rites. (*Suppl.*, 37,1,ad2) Although the Council of Trent studiously avoided these disputed points among the scholastics, theologians today all but universally hold that episcopacy is a distinct order from that of priesthood and that it is conferred in a strict sacramental rite. The majority also hold that the subdiaconate and minor orders are sacramentals and not part of the sacrament of order. As regards the unity of the sacrament, St. Thomas' principle appears to be valid, but in keeping with what has been said, the fullness of the priesthood and the sacrament of order is to be found in episcopal consecration and by way of participation in presbyteral and diaconal ordination.

### *Development of the Rites*

The early rites of ordination were quite simple, an imposition of hands and an appropriate prayer invoking the power of the Holy Spirit. In the early thirteenth century, various ceremonies were added in the Western Church to symbolize more graphically the office and functions of the ordinand. Thus, in addition to the imposition of hands, the candidate for priesthood received from the bishop a chalice and a paten to symbolize more clearly his sacrificial functions. From the time of St. Thomas most theologians regarded this *traditio instrumentorum* as the essential matter or part of the essential matter of the sacrament of order, a view which was confirmed in an *Instruction for the Armenians,* drawn up at the time of the Council of Florence, 1439. (Cf. D701.) A recent decision of the Holy See, however, has decided that, at least for the future, the essential matter of the sacrament of order is the imposition of hands alone. (See p. 68.)

## THE REFORMATION AND TRENT

### *Teaching of the Reformers*

Repeatedly in his writings Luther insisted that all Christians are priests, a dignity which meant very little since Luther had denied the sacrificial character of the sacrament of the Lord's supper. All Christians were priests but they could exercise their priesthood only in the temple of their own souls. Their priesthood could not be given expression in the sacrifice of the Mass. According to Luther, the function of the ordained priest or minister was to administer the sacraments and to preach the word of God. He who failed to preach forfeited his priesthood. Theoretically all Christians are qualified to administer the sacraments and to preach, but for reasons of propriety and order certain individuals are appointed by the community to perform these offices. Those so appointed or ordained do not possess any powers which are not possessed by the laity.

Calvin's teaching is not basically different from that of Luther, although Calvin does demand a special call or vocation from God which the Christian community will test under the interior light of the Spirit before the candidate is officially appointed for the ministry. The Anglican *Thirty-Nine Articles of Religion* do not regard ordination as a sacrament instituted by Christ. Anglicans, however, have always placed much store in the rite of episcopal ordination, which for them continues the apostolic Succession in their Church. Yet in defending the validity of Anglican orders, most Anglicans speak of their ordinations as though they were sacramental rites. (See p. 68.)

## *Teaching of Trent*

The Council of Trent is concerned principally with the Christian priesthood, a dignity and office which is held in common by bishops and priests. It defines that bishops are superior to priests and that they have powers which simple priests do not share, namely the power to confirm and to ordain. (*Session* 23, Can. 7, D967) It also defines that the hierarchy of bishops, presbyters, and deacons was instituted by divine arrangement (Can. 6, D966), but refrains from stating that these orders are all of divine institution or that episcopal consecration is part of the sacrament of order. In fact, when Trent speaks of order as a sacrament which imprints a character it has in mind only the sacrament of priesthood, neither affirming nor denying the sacramentality of the episcopacy and the other orders, major and minor. A summary of other points in Trent's teaching follows:

(1) The Christian priesthood was instituted by Christ (ch. 1, D957), and confers on the recipient the power to consecrate and to offer the true body and blood of the Lord, and the power to forgive and to retain sins. The priestly ministry is not restricted merely to preaching the gospel, nor do priests who fail to preach cease to be priests. (Can. 1, D961)

(2) In order that the priestly ministry be celebrated more worthily and with greater dignity, there exist in the Church other orders which are at the service of the priesthood. These are the orders of deacon, subdeacon, acolyte, exorcist, reader, and porter. The subdiaconate is one of the major orders. (ch. 2, D958) These other orders, both major and minor are, as it were, grades or steps leading to the priesthood. (Can. 2, D962)

(3) Order or ordination is a true and proper sacrament instituted by Christ and is not merely a rite of choosing ministers of the word of God and of the sacraments. (ch. 3, Can. 3, D959, 963)

(4) Through sacred ordination the Holy Spirit is given and a character is impressed. He who is once ordained cannot become a layman. (Can. 4, D964)

## MORE RECENT QUESTIONS

### *Anglican Orders*

The question of the validity of Anglican Orders was officially closed by Leo XIII in his encyclical *Apostolicae Curae,* in which he declared "that ordinations carried out according to the Anglican rite have been and are absolutely null and utterly void." (D1966) It was the pontiff's contention that the Anglican rite of orders, by eliminating from the old Catholic rite all reference to sacrifice, made it clear that the purpose of the new rite was to ordain ministers of the word and not Catholic priests, and that those who use this rite express externally—whatever their subjective intention or belief—not what the Church does but what the reformers were doing in fact, namely, ordaining ministers of the word and the sacraments. Accordingly, the Anglican rite is defective in form as well as defective in external intention.

### *The Matter and Form of Orders*

As already noted (p. 66) many theologians agreed with St. Thomas that the essential matter of the sacrament of order consisted, in whole or in part, in the ceremony of handing over or of touching the sacred objects which symbolize the office of the one being ordained (*traditio instrumentorum*). Without deciding the speculative question as to what constituted the matter and form of orders in the past, Pius XII decided that for the future, "the matter of the sacred orders of diaconate, priesthood and episcopate is the imposition of hands, and it alone; the form, and again alone, are the words which determine the application of this matter, words which express the sacramental effects, namely, the power of order and the grace of the Spirit, and which the Church accepts and uses as such." (*Apostolic Constitution on Sacred Orders,* Nov. 30, 1947; *AAS* 40 [1958], 2f)

## THE POWER AND GRACE OF ORDER

Like the sacraments of baptism and confirmation the sacrament of order confers a permanent and indelible character in virtue of which the sacrament cannot be repeated. The fullness of the priestly character is conferred in the ordination of the bishop and by way of participation in the presbyter or simple priest. In virtue of the episcopal character, there is brought to completion the fullness of Christ's priestly ministry which he is to continue. In the formula of episcopal consecration the Church asks: "Bring to completion in your priest the fullness of your ministry." In virtue of the character the bishop is configured or likened to Christ in his threefold priestly role as priest, prophet, and king. As priest, the bishop has the power to offer the eucharistic sacrifice and to forgive sins. As prophet, he has the office *ex officio* of teaching and preaching. As king he has the full pastoral charge of guiding the flock entrusted to his care. For this office the bishop is consecrated, and to equip him for his ministry special charisms or graces are given.

The presbyter, on the other hand, is ordained to assist the bishop, just as the seventy elders or presbyters of the Old Law were selected to assist Moses in governing the chosen people of God; and to equip them for this office they shared in the grace given to Moses. (See p. 63.) In the present ordination formula for priesthood, the candidate is ordained to assist the bishop as a fellow worker (*cooperator*) in the priestly ministry. However, his ministry is dependent upon that of his own bishop or that bishop ordinary with whom he is laboring. In virtue of the powers received in his ordination the simple priest can consecrate validly and offer the eucharistic sacrifice, but his priestly ministry is unlawful unless he is in "good standing" with his bishop. For the rest of his priestly ministry he needs either jurisdiction or authorization to act validly. Thus, to hear confessions and to preach he must have jurisdiction or "faculties" from the bishop. To confirm he must have authorization from Rome, which is given to pastors, chaplains, and other priests of the Western rites, if no Catholic bishop is available. (Cf. *AAS*, 38 [Sept. 1946], 349–358.)

Whether a simple priest can ordain others to the priesthood is a question disputed by Catholic theologians. There are four recorded instances of individual popes of the fifteenth century granting to priest-abbots of the Cistercian Order permission to ordain their subjects to the diaconate and even to the priesthood. (Documents in Appendix of H. Lennerz' *De Sacramento Ordinis,* ed. 2, Romae, 1953) True, the Council of Trent states clearly that simple priests have no power to confirm or to ordain, but in the case of confirmation this can only mean without episcopal or papal authorization. (See p. 67.) Hence it is not inconceivable that priests have the same radical sacramental powers as bishops, although for some sacraments the valid exercise of these powers is dependent on the local bishop or the bishop of Rome.

Some theologians have appealed to the priest's basic power to confirm and to ordain as proof that the bishop is distinguished from the simple priest not in virtue of the sacrament of order, but in virtue of his jurisdiction, a view which St. Thomas seems to have held. But this view is hardly tenable in the light of Pope Pius XII's teaching that the form of order should express for the episcopate, the presbyterate, and the diaconate "the *sacramental* effects, namely the power of order and the grace of the Spirit" (emphasis added). Hence the bishop is distinguished from the simple priest in virtue of the special sacramental power and grace which he receives in the sacrament of order. Reference to the "grace of the Spirit" brings us to the grace of order.

The specific grace of order is to make the recipient a worthy minister of his office. (*Instruction for the Armenians,* D701) In the ordination of Timothy to the episcopate, Paul mentions the spirit of "power, love, and self-discipline," graces which sanctify and enrich the recipient and assist him in his service to the Church. In the early centuries, when presbyters rarely celebrated the eucharist or preached, the special grace asked for presbyters was the grace of good example, a grace closely related to the spirit of self-discipline or sobriety of which Paul speaks. Even today the formula of priestly ordination in the Roman Pontifical prays for the "spirit of holiness, that he may . . . gently reproach the conduct of others by the example of his holiness." The "preface" of priestly ordination asks that "the beauty of perfect justice may shine in them, and that they be prudent fellow workers of the bishop." A later prayer begs that they "may set an example of justice, steadfastness, mercy, fortitude, and all other virtues." Among these "other virtues," and closely associated with the virtue of sobriety or self-discipline is the difficult virtue of chastity which merits special consideration under the heading "priestly celibacy."

A SUPPLEMENT

# PRIESTLY CELIBACY

When God promised through Moses to make a new covenant with the Israelites on Sinai, Moses was instructed to prepare the people beforehand. Part of this preparation was the proscription that the menfolk were "to touch no woman" for the space of two days. (Cf. Ex 19,14.15.) When David asked Abimelech for bread for himself and his soldiers, the priest replied: "There is no ordinary bread in my possession, but there is holy bread, if only the young men have kept themselves from women." (1 Sm 21,4) This demand of recent continence on the part of those who approached God or ate of bread consecrated to the Lord suggests that there was a basic connection between periodic celibacy and the service of God. The Jewish priesthood was hereditary, the priestly office having been transferred from father to son within the priestly tribe of Levi. There is no thought of a celibate priesthood among the Jews, unless we consider the priests of the Essene communities, such as those at Qumrân, who seem to have been celibates. But in the Mosaic dispensation, where priests were continued in their sons, the priest was expected to observe continence during the period in which he served in the Temple.

The Christian priesthood is not hereditary. The priesthood of Christ is continued not by carnal descent, but solely by the grace of the sacrament of order. Again, the service of the Christian priest is not periodic but continuous in the daily sacrifice of Christians in the eucharistic liturgy. For these and other reasons to be seen, it is understandable why continued continence or celibacy has always been upheld as an ideal of the Christian priesthood, and why, in the course of time, it was made obligatory on bishops, priests, and deacons preparing for the priesthood in the Church of the West. The ideal of celibacy is encouraged by Christ in his public ministry, and suggested strongly by St. Paul, though in a context of eschatological expectation. (1 Cor 7)

*New Testament Witness.* The first apostles and disciples of Jesus were mostly married men, naturally enough, because of the Jewish view of the excellence of marriage. It would seem, however, that quite early in Christ's ministry the married men among them severed family ties. Thus, Peter, acting as spokesman for the Twelve, said to the Lord: "Behold, we have left all and followed you." And Jesus said to them: "Amen, I say to you, there is no one who has left house, or parents, or brothers, or wife, or children, for the sake of the kingdom of God, who shall not receive much more in the present age, and in the age to come life everlasting." (Lk 18,28–30) Again, in answer to the apostle's reaction to our Lord's severe teaching on divorce and remarriage—teaching which in fact reduced a man married to a wife who has left him for an adulterous union to the status of the celibate—Jesus spoke not only of enforced celibacy but of celibacy freely undertaken for the kingdom of heaven. "And there are eunuchs who have made themselves so for the kingdom of heaven's sake. Let him accept it who can." (Mt 19,12; and see p. 86.)

In his teaching on virginity and marriage in response to specific questions of the community at Corinth, St. Paul exhorts, without commanding, the unmarried to remain as they are: "But I say to the unmarried and to widows, it is good for them if they so remain even as I." (I Cor 7,8) The reason given is not that of self-abnegation but of dedication to God. "He who is unmarried is concerned about the things of the Lord, how he may please God." (1 Cor 7,32) St. Paul was aware that the early Christian hierarchy would be drawn principally from older and more established men in the community, but in his instructions to Timothy and Titus he writes that candidates for the episcopate and/or the presbyterate must be men of one wife. Widows and widowers were free to remarry, but not so the candidate for the office of bishop or presbyter. (Cf. 1 Tim 3,2; Tit 1,6.) The same ruling applies to candidates for the diaconate. (Cf. 1 Tim 3,12.)

*Early Development.* Celibacy as an ecclesiastical institution obligatory on clerics was established only over a comparatively long period of time. Time and changing circumstances were required for its widespread realization, and even then it made its way in the East chiefly in virtue of its association with monasticism. In the early centuries, many bishops, priests, and deacons were ordained after their marriage, and there was no law forbidding them to continue their marital relations. Yet even before the influence of monasticism and the ascetic ideal of continence, many among the Catholic clergy found the grace to espouse the celibate life. Making allowance for Tertullian's puritanical leanings, there is no reason to suspect him as a witness when he writes, about the year 210: "How many you see in sacred orders who have embraced continence, who have preferred to be wedded to God!" (*Exhortation to Chastity,* 13) In the middle of the third century Origen commends the continence of Jewish priests during the period of their service in the Temple, but he finds even greater observance of the virtue of continence in priests of the New Law: "In the Church too priests also can have children, but in the manner of him who said: 'My children, I suffer for you the pangs of childbirth in order that Christ might be formed in you.'" (*On Leviticus,* 6,6) There is a suggestion here that celibacy was already enforced on the clergy in certain sections of the Church. But the law of celibacy was by no means universal, if there was such a law.

*Celibacy in the West.* At the Council of Elvira in Spain (c. 305), it was enacted that bishops, priests, and deacons who were married must live in continence and renounce all marital relations. (Cf. D52c.) In 386 a Council of Rome, the decisions of which were promulgated by Pope St. Siricius in Africa, Gaul, and Spain, deplored the fact that many priests and deacons, contrary to ecclesiastical discipline, were begetting children, either by their own wives or outside of wedlock. These clerics had evidently appealed to the practice of priests of the Old Law, but as the council notes: "They forget that Christ, without annulling the Old Law, came to perfect it." (D89) At about the same time (391), St. Ambrose of Milan notes that many priests in outlying districts were married and raising families. They too had appealed to the Old Law. Ambrose reminds them that even the Jewish priests were obliged to abstain from their wives for a few days before offering sacrifice, a practice which even the Christian laity follows before approaching the eucharistic sacrifice. Ambrose then concludes: "If in the time of figure, the discipline was so exacting, how much more exacting ought it to be now that the Truth has come." (*On the Office of Ministers,* 1,50)

By the end of the fourth century obligatory celibacy was well established in the Church of the West. St. Augustine was aware of the severe demands made upon clerics of his day, but he can point to their heroism as an example for husbands who are constrained by the law of God to remain continent if they have divorced their wives for infidelity. His own approach in exhorting such men to continence follows:

> Therefore we say to them: Look now, suppose the forceful entreaties of the people should oblige you to assume their office [i.e., of clerics], would you not carry out the obligations of chastity, once they were assumed? . . . For if many of God's ministers have accepted what has been imposed quite suddenly and unexpectedly in the hope that they will shine with greater brilliance in Christ's inheritance, how much more should you avoid adultery and live continently, not out of fear that you may shine less brilliantly in the kingdom of God but that you may burn in the gehenna of fire. (*On Adulterous Marriages,* 2,22)

During the early Middle Ages the celibate ideal was in great measure lost, to the detriment not only of the clerical state but to the state of marriage. No longer could the Church appeal, as in the past, to the example of her priests to stem the tide of divorce that threatened to undermine Christian marriage and the family. Reform measures were repeatedly introduced, but it was not until the great reform under St. Gregory VII (Hildebrand), in the eleventh century, that a successful stand was made against clerical incontinence and laxity in marriage observance.

In the first Council of the Lateran (1123), priests, deacons, and bishops were forbidden, under penalty, to live with their wives or concubines. (Cf. D360.) The second Council of the Lateran (1139) went a step further by declaring that marriages contracted by clerics in major orders were not only unlawful but invalid, a declaration which was made anew by the Council of Trent some four centuries later. (Cf. D979.)

The law of clerical celibacy was not seriously challenged in the West until the time of Martin Luther. Admittedly, celibacy was honored in the breach almost as much as in the observance, and the morals of the clergy stood in need of drastic reform. Luther, however, introduced no reform in this matter. Instead, he regarded virginity and celibacy as unnatural, and the vows of virginity and celibacy as sins of presumption rather than acts of virtue. Just prior to his own marriage to the former nun Katherine Bora (1525), Luther had arrived at the conviction that marriage was a command of God as well as a demand of nature. He went so far as to regard it as a terrible thing that a man should face God on the day of judgment without a wife: "I made you a man, not to stand alone but to take a wife; where is your wife?" ("To Albert, Archbishop of Mainz," June 2, 1525, in *Letters,* ed. by De Wette, 2, 676) Luther's repeated insistence on the impossibility of a life of continence explains much of his teaching on the question of divorce and remarriage. For history proves that the Christian ideal of indissoluble marriage stands or falls with the esteem in which celibacy is held as a way of life. Against Luther's naturalism and pessimism the Council of Trent not only defined that celibacy and virginity are "more perfect" states than that of marriage; it extended the decision of the second Lateran Council by declaring that marriages attempted by those solemnly professed as well as those in sacred orders are invalid. (Cf. D979, 980.)

*Celibacy in the East.* At the first Council of Nicaea (325) an attempt was made to impose continence on bishops, priests, and deacons in accord with the earlier decision of the Spanish Council of Elvira (305). The Church historian Socrates tells us that bishop Paphnucius, although himself a celibate, rose in the assembly and objected to an enactment which he considered too harsh and rigorous. He believed that it was enough that candidates for these offices should forego marriage in accord with ancient tradition, but that those already married at the time of ordination should not be forced to separate from their wives. Not only would such legislation be harsh but it would give the impression that the Church regarded marriage as evil instead of sacred.

This latter observation had particular relevance in the Church of the East, where Gnosticism and Encratism were strong, and where many regarded marriage and, more particularly the use of marriage, as evil. (See p. 89.) In any event, the arguments of Paphnucius prevailed and seem to have influenced Eastern legislation on the question of clerical celibacy. Such legislation became comparatively fixed in the Eastern Synod or Council "in Trullo" of Constantinople (692). Subdeacons may not marry. Deacons and presbyters, if already married, are not to separate from their wives, except during the period when they exercise their sacred functions. Bishops are to practice perfect continence. The wife of one who becomes a bishop is to retire to a monastery at some distance. However, the bishop ought to provide for her, and if she is worthy she can be named a deaconess. (Can. 6,13,48)

In the Eastern Orthodox Churches today, subdeacons are allowed to marry and to continue on to priesthood without separating from their wives, a permission which most Orthodox clerics use during their subdiaconate. In the new code of Canon Law prepared for Eastern Catholics, 
the subdiaconate along with major orders has been made a diriment (i.e.,

invalidating) impediment to marriage. (Can. 70) Where there is a shortage of priests for Eastern Catholics, as in Canada and the United States where immigration has been heavy, married men may, with special dispensation from their own patriarch or bishop, be ordained to the priesthood. (Cf. *Code of Oriental Canon Law,* translation and commentary by V. Pospishil, Ford City, Pa., 1960, pp. 67–70.)

*Doctrinal Significance.* The advantages of priestly celibacy from the spiritual and apostolic points of view are many and compelling (see pp. 106ff), but they are all somewhat relative and fail to explain the essential significance of ecclesiastical celibacy. A wife and family can be a hindrance and distraction in the work of the ministry, but there have been countless instances where individuals have been able to combine the two vocations of marriage and the ministry without prejudice to either. It would be out of order to attempt to establish a *necessary* bond between celibacy and priesthood. Yet we hope to show that celibacy as it developed in the Church of the West is wholly in conformity with the intentions of Christ for some members of his Church, and that the reasons which led the Church to enforce it on her priests and those preparing for the priesthood are not only utilitarian but theologically significant.

Every vow of chastity expresses the individual's complete surrender and dedication to Christ. Again, the vows of chastity taken by religious men and women are an eschatological sign of the kingdom of heaven where there will be no marriage. Such vows are then a constant witness to the reality of the life to come. "For at the resurrection they will neither marry nor be given in marriage, but will be as angels of God in heaven." (Mt. 22,30) For these and other reasons, Christians of the East and the West have always regarded celibacy and virginity as the "more perfect" state. That this is true was defined against Protestant denials by the Council of Trent in its decree on marriage. (See p. 94.)

The commitment to celibacy made by those in sacred orders has special significance. It is not only a personal commitment and complete surrender to Christ. It is a surrender to Christ's spouse the Church. The act has social or ecclesial overtones. It is not only a witness to the reality of the life to come, but to the present situation as well. This is seen particularly in the celibacy of the bishop, and explains why from the earliest times a bishop was not to remarry after his wife's death; why, if married, he was to separate from her; and why, even in the Orthodox Eastern churches today, a bishop is drawn from the unmarried clergy. The bishop is in effect the image of the Father. His only children will be the members of the Church entrusted to his care. As the image of Christ, his only bride will be the Church to which he is wedded. When simple priests or presbyters began to share more fully in the functions of the bishop, when to them was entrusted a portion of the Church, it is understandable why the priest too was called upon to give himself over to the Church fully in this symbolic way. The universal Church has never called in question, however, the validity of commitment of the married men who, by reason of immemorial custom in the East, ask and receive major orders.

CHAPTER FOUR

# THE SACRAMENT OF MARRIAGE

In the opening paragraph of the encyclical *Casti Connubii* (On Christian Marriage), Pope Pius XI identifies the dignity of marriage under these three headings: (1) God is the author of marriage; (2) Christ restored marriage to its primitive dignity as the permanent and exclusive union of one man and one woman; (3) Christ raised marriage to the rank of a true and great sacrament of the New Law. This teaching of the encyclical repeats the teaching of Trent and furnishes us with an outline of the main doctrinal points on marriage. The divine institution of marriage, its decline from the divine ideal with the fall of man, its restoration by Christ, and something of its sacredness which suggests its sacramentality, are found in both testaments of Scripture.

## MARRIAGE IN THE OLD TESTAMENT

### *Divine Institution and Purpose*

The Book of Genesis twice relates the creation of man. In the first account stress is placed on creativeness or procreation as the purpose of marriage as instituted by God and blessed by him: "And God said, Let us make man to our own image and likeness. And God created man to his own image; to the image of God he created them, and God blessed them saying: Increase and multiply, and fill the earth." (Gn 1,26–28) Such is the account of the Priestly author.

In the second or Yahwist account the stress is on the natural inclination of man and woman to form a union that is permanent and exclusive, with the idea latent that the woman is drawn from the man and that the latter finds fulfillment again in being joined to a woman: "It is not good for man to be alone; let us make him a helpmate like unto himself." In this telling of the mystery of marriage, after God has fashioned the woman Eve from the side of Adam, the man exclaims: "This now is bone of my bone and flesh of my flesh," at which point the inspired author interrupts his narrative to say: "Wherefore a man shall leave father and mother and shall cleave to his wife; and they shall be two in one flesh." (Gn 2,18.23.24) Christ will appeal to the observation of the sacred author as to the words of the Spirit of God (Mt 19,5), as part of his continual assumption that all Scripture is divinely inspired.

From the second account of creation, the pattern or nature of marriage in the Hebrew revelation is sufficiently clear. A man will be led by nature to form an exclusive and permanent union with a woman, a union so exclusive that he will be prepared, if need be, to sever the closest bonds that bind him to his parents, in order to cleave to his wife. The revelation is not given in technical terms of the unity and the indissolubility of the marriage bond, of course, but the expression "cleave to" implies much more than a casual union. The further expression "two in one flesh" implies a union that is so intimate as to preclude an interloper or a third party.

### *Marriage and the Fall of Man*

The story of Adam's sin of disobedience contains an explanation of the loss of the creature's friendship with his Creator, and of the loss of perfect harmony in his faculties whereby he had been completely open to his fellow creatures, notably his marriage partner. Catholic theology speaks of this imbalance as the loss of integrity or wholeness. The sex instinct is no longer perfectly under reason's control. Sheerly sensitive appetites are not subject to the higher faculties, and a part result of this is shame: the consciousness that the body can rebel against the spirit. Shame stems from the experience of an evil tendency within, which can forestall reason, which can lead man into evil; it is the premonition of a discord that can shatter our inner harmony even further.

Temptation, if it was to come to man in his condition of harmony, had to strike at his spirit. The sacred author describes the first temptation as the desire "to be as gods, knowing good and evil." (Gn 3,5) After the sin of disobedience, the man and the woman "knew evil." They experienced in themselves not only the guilt of sin but also the evil of concupiscence, itself not a sin, but a proneness toward sin. They realized as they had not before, that sex could be divisive, that it could seek its gratification apart from the controlling influence of the spirit, that sex could seek its object in a body, in any body, and that it could cease to be the physical expression of love of a person. Sex could degenerate into lust, and lust is promiscuous. But promiscuity is inherently opposed to the permanent and exclusive character of marriage.

The biblical account of marriage is one of progressive departure from the divine pattern of marriage. Among the descendants of Cain, the "first murderer," is Lamech, the first to be mentioned as a bigamist. (Gn 4,19) Scripture records that Lamech was a murderer as well. Just prior to the account of the deluge, a scrap of ancient narrative is introduced which describes what appear to be promiscuous unions between the "sons of God" and the "daughters of men." (Gn 6,2) The reason given for the deluge is that, "The earth was corrupted before God and filled with iniquity." (Gn 6,11) In the deluge, four families are saved. It is worthy of note that all are monogamous, Noah and his wife, and Noah's three sons and daughters-in-law. (Gn. 7,13)

### *Marriage in Ancient Israel*



Polygamy is so normal among pastoral peoples of the "fertile crescent" in the second millennium B.C. that Abraham, the father of the Hebrew people, does not hesitate to accept from Sara, his sterile wife, Agar, a slave wife, that he may produce offspring. Pope Pius XI in his encyclical *Casti Connubii,* (n.20) adopts the view that God granted Abraham and succeeding patriarchs a dispensation from the primitive law of monogamy, but Leo XIII speaks of a mere toleration of polygamy and divorce among the Israelites, not an exemption from the law in the strict sense of the term. The passage from Leo is worth quoting. His concern is doctrinal, and is not particularly related to the cultural history of the period. Speaking of marriage as divinely instituted, he says:

> This form of marriage, however, so excellent and so preeminent, began to be corrupted by degrees and to disappear among the heathens; and became among the Jewish race flouted and in a measure obscured. For in their midst a common custom was gradually introduced by which it was accounted as lawful for a man to have more than one wife; and eventually when, by reason of the hardness of their hearts, Moses indulgently permitted them to put away their wives, the way was open to divorce. (*Arcanum Divinae Sapientiae,* ed. Wynne, p. 60f)

Most theologians are inclined to view polygamy and divorce among the Israelites as abuses tolerated for a time rather than dispensations or exemptions from the primitive law of monogamy and indissolubility. This appears to be true of the Mosaic legislation on polygamy and divorce. Moses legislated within the framework of established custom. He did not abolish custom but legislated against many of the abuses connected with polygamy and divorce.

## *Mosaic Legislation*

POLYGAMY Moses foresees the possibility of a man having two or more wives; the second wife will normally be a slave wife. But even she will have certain privileges. For a month she will be permitted to mourn her parents. During this period she is to remain untouched by her captor. If after this period she does not please her master, he may not whip her or sell her for money. If he takes her to wife, her children will enjoy the same rights as the principal wife. Her firstborn, if the firstborn of the husband, will have the right of primogeniture or inheritance. (Cf. Dt 21,10–17.)

DIVORCE In the Mosaic teaching on divorce, there is a serious attempt to root out the evil by making it more difficult to repudiate one's wife. A good reason had to be established—something shameful in the woman; a bill of divorce had to be written and delivered into her hands. Finally, if the divorced woman married again she could never return to her first husband. (Cf. Dt 24,1–4.) In this way a man would have to think twice before divorcing his wife.

CONCLUSION This may seem feeble legislation to the Catholic Christian, but considering the moral codes of surrounding societies and the longstanding customs of the "wandering Aramean" (Cf. Dt 26,5) who was Israel's father, it was an amazing piece of regulatory prescription. The ideal of monogamy and indissolubility was never allowed to be lost. After Moses, the prophets repeatedly use the ideal marriage as the symbol of God's marriage to Israel. (Cf. Is 54,4–8; 62,4f; Jer 2,1–3; Os 2,16–19; 3,1–3.) Malachia, last of the inspired books of the prophets, prepares the way for the teaching of Christ when he warns the Jewish people that God hates divorce: "Did he not make one being, with flesh and spirit: and what does the one require but godly offspring? You must then safeguard life that is your own, and not break faith with the wife of your youth. For I hate divorce, says the Lord God of Israel." (Mal 2,15f)

## MARRIAGE IN THE NEW TESTAMENT

In Jesus' time, polygamy had become a luxury among the Jews, chiefly for economic reasons. This fact probably explains why there is no explicit reference to polygamy in the New Testament. However, divorce was quite prevalent, justified as it was by the Mosaic legislation which permitted divorce if something "shameful" were discovered in the wife. At the time of Christ, the "shameful" thing was interpreted by the more rigorous school of Shammai to be moral uncleanness or adultery; the laxer school of Hillel saw in the phrase of Dt 24,1ff anything displeasing in the wife, even to lack of comeliness or lack of culinary skill. It is against this background that we can understand Jesus' teaching on divorce, and indirectly on polygamy.

### *The Teaching of Christ*

At the beginning of his public ministry Jesus performed his first "sign" of changing water into wine at a wedding feast. Undoubtedly the symbolism of Israel's nuptials with Yahweh was uppermost in the use St. John's gospel makes of this miracle, a secondary theme being the supplanting of the water of the Jewish purificatory rite by the "new wine" of Jesus' doctrine. Many Fathers of the Church see in Christ's action a transformation not only of water into wine but of the natural state of marriage into something sacred and sanctifying. (See p. 92.) In his sermon on the mount, which almost certainly summarizes a later encounter with the scribes and pharisees on the subject of divorce, Jesus makes it clear that the primitive law of Genesis still obtains, and that a man who divorces his wife, unless she is already guilty of adultery, causes her to commit adultery. Accordingly, a man who marries a divorced woman—there is no qualification of this in the parallel places of Mark and Luke, therefore for any reason whatever—is guilty of adultery. "But I say to you that everyone who puts away his wife, save on account of immorality, causes her to commit adultery; and he who marries a woman who is put away commits adultery." (Mt 5,31f) In this passage there is question of putting away a woman guilty of immorality (*porneía*). There is no suggestion that the innocent husband may remarry. In fact, the marriage bond is still presumed to exist, since a woman put away cannot be taken by another man without committing the sin of adultery.

In a later passage of Matthew and in the parallel passages from Mark and Luke mentioned above, we have the actual encounter of Jesus with his critics which prompted his teaching on the permanence or indissolubility of marriage. The setting or context is best given in Mt 19,3–12. The Master's critics approach him as a rabbi asking him to decide the question: "Is it lawful for a man to put away his wife *for any cause*," (emphasis added), a provocative reference to the teaching of the school of Hillel. Instead of deciding a point of Mosaic Law disputed by the schools of Hillel and Shammai, Jesus avoids the trap set for him by transcending the question. He does not take sides in the dispute, but appeals to another text in Scripture: "Have you not read that the Creator from the beginning made them male and female and said 'For this cause a man shall leave his father and mother, and cleave to his wife and the two shall become one flesh?' Therefore now they are no longer two, but one flesh. What therefore God has joined together, let no man put asunder."

The pharisees have been answered, and on terms quite different from what they thought was the one certainty in the case, namely the text of Dt 24,1ff. Probably genuinely shocked at his response, they show their hand and the motive behind their original question: "Why then did Moses command to give a bill of divorce and to put her away?"

Christ's reply is first a corrective and then a reaffirmation of what he had already said: "Moses by reason of the hardness of your hearts permitted you to put away your wives, but from the beginning it was not so." (Mt 19,3–8; cf. Mk 10,2–9.)

At this point, the pharisees leave Jesus, and the question is resumed by his disciples. (Cf. Mk 10,10.) If our Lord allowed any exception to the law of indissolubility in the context of Matthew's gospel, both his own disciples and the pharisees seem unaware of it. In fact, he would have deceived them in citing the law of Genesis against the law of Moses unless he meant to indicate a clear difference. The permission of divorce for the reason of adultery would have constituted no difference whatever; it would simply have put him in the camp of Shammai. This would have served to prolong the discussion, on the pharisees' original terms, and it would have made Jesus' disciples' subsequent objection to his teaching meaningless. Note that our Lord did not change or soften his teaching when taking up the question with his disciples.

Luke quotes Jesus as saying: "Everyone who puts away his wife and marries another commits adultery; and he who marries a woman who has been put away from her husband commits adultery." (Lk 16,18) Mark's gospel, with an eye to Roman civil practice which allowed a woman to divorce her husband, is equally certain that our Lord's teaching on the matter of divorce was unequivocal and allowed of no exceptions: "And in the house, his disciples again asked him concerning this. And he said to them, 'Whoever puts away his wife and marries another commits adultery against her; and if the wife puts away her husband and marries another, she commits adultery.'" (Mk 10,11.12)

ADULTERY AGAINST A WOMAN The idea of adultery against a woman was as foreign to the Jews as it is incompatible with all codes of law which allow polygamy. In such codes, the wife is the property of the man. Adultery is the violation of the husband's rights over his wife or wives. To commit adultery *against a woman* implies that the wife has rights which can be violated by her husband's relations with another woman, whether the other woman is married or single. This principle is something absolutely new in Christianity and distinctive of it. It explains what, basically, is meant by the Christian emancipation of woman. St. Paul expresses the principle in the strongest of terms when he says: "The wife has not authority over her body, but the husband; the husband likewise has not authority over his body, but the wife." (1 Cor 7,4) Marriage is a surrender of self, of the rights to one's body. To give one's self to another after those rights have been given over to the wife is adultery on the part of the husband against his wife. Accordingly, polygamy, as well as divorce, is adultery against the first wife.

THE EXCEPTIVE CLAUSE IN MT 19,9 In the general context of Mt 19,3–8, and in Mk 10,2–12, Lk 16,18, and in 1 Cor 7,4, it is inconceivable that Christ should introduce an exception which would allow a man to divorce his wife and to remarry. Yet our Lord seems to make such an exception in the famous clause of Mt 19,9: "And I say to you, that whoever puts away his wife, except for immorality (*porneía*), and marries another, commits adultery." It would seem that Christ here retreats from the position taken against the pharisees to assume a position which is not radically different from that of Shammai, who allowed divorce and remarriage only on grounds of immorality of the part of the wife. Since such an interpretation does violence to the context, exegetes, both Protestant and Catholic, have sought an explanation of the exceptive clause. Various interpretations have been given, a number of which follow:

(1) The exceptive clause allows remarriage in the case of adultery but the exception was introduced by Matthew to accommodate Christ's teaching to the needs of Jewish converts. Christ taught the ideal of indissolubility—an ideal, however, which would have to yield at times to the hard facts of life. This is not a Catholic approach to the exceptive clause. Catholics can admit an inspired gloss or interpolation on the part of Matthew, but not one that would falsify or change Christ's teaching. Again, Christ is hardly speaking of the Christian ideal when he brands divorce and remarriage as adultery. His teaching on the indissolubility of marriage is one of strict precept and not of evangelical counsel.

(2) The exceptive clause is an inspired gloss of Matthew, but immorality or uncleanness (*porneía*) means uncleanness in the legal sense of marrying within the forbidden degrees of kinship, a gloss which was inserted to conform with the decision of the council at Jerusalem to retain the Jewish dietary laws and their laws governing *porneía* or incest. Thus gentile converts "are to abstain from anything that has been contaminated by idols, and from immorality (*porneía*), from anything strangled, and from blood." (Ac 15,20) Accordingly, a man who puts away his wife, unless he finds his marriage to be unlawful, and marries again, is guilty of adultery. This is the more common interpretation of Catholic exegetes today. It finds further support in Paul's excommunication of a Corinthian who is guilty of incest (*porneía*), i.e., marriage to his father's wife. (1 Cor 5,1)

(3) The clause "and marries again" in conjunction with the exceptive clause is an uninspired gloss or interpolation of an early fourth century copyist. The combined clauses are not found in all manuscripts, nor are they so cited by any writer of the ante-Nicene period in discussing the question of divorce. In fact, for the first four centuries the question of allowing divorce and remarriage on scriptural grounds was not even discussed. This view commends itself to the author and merits more consideration than it has received.

(4) Immorality, i.e., adultery, in the wife is reason for separation (an imperfect divorce) but not for remarriage. This has been the general view of the Fathers of the Church from the time that the present reading of Mt 19,9 became the received text. The text has been so interpreted by Augustine, Jerome, and the Fathers of the West generally.

REACTION OF CHRIST'S DISCIPLES "If the case of a man with his wife is so, it is not expedient to marry." (Mt 19,10) This reaction of the disciples makes sense only on the supposition that Christ ruled out remarriage even in the case of an adulterous wife. The disciples are in fact implying that our Lord's rigorous teaching will demand celibacy in certain instances, chiefly when there is adultery in the wife. A husband might put up with other defects in his wife, but public opinion if not conscience would force him to put away, at least secretly, an adulterous wife. This would force him to lead the life of a celibate. Christ does not deny that this may be the result of his teaching on divorce but takes the opportunity to treat of celibacy, sometimes enforced on a man, which is also freely embraced for religious reasons: "There are eunuchs who have made themselves so for the kingdom of heaven. Let him accept it who can." (Mt 19,12)

CONCLUSION According to Christ's teaching there is no reason which will justify a man in divorcing his wife and remarrying, no reason which will justify a woman in divorcing her husband and remarrying. To this extent marriage is intrinsically indissoluble; it cannot be dissolved by the contracting parties. Whether or not marriage can be dissolved by civil society or by the Church—in which case marriage would be extrinsically dissoluble—is not discussed by Christ. The question had no pertinence at the time. In Roman society marriage could be dissolved by mutual consent, and in Jewish society by the action of the husband in giving his wife a bill of divorce. The Church denies that the state has received authority from God to dissolve any marriage. "What God has joined let no man put asunder." The Church, however, claims that she has received authority from God to dissolve, for good reasons, a marriage contracted by non-Christians, or, if contracted by Christians (*ratum*), a marriage which has not been sealed by intercourse (*non-consummatum*). But this question will be discussed later.

## *The Teaching of St. Paul*

Christ's teaching on divorce and the moral excellence of celibacy or virginity freely embraced for the kingdom of God is repeated by St. Paul in 1 Cor 7. The dignity of marriage as a symbol or sacrament of Christ's union with his Church, together with the obligations which follow for Christians, is developed in Eph 5. Both chapters have shaped and continue to control Catholic teaching on marriage, virginity, and divorce.

1 COR 7 In 1 Corinthians Paul is concerned with the *parousía* or coming of the Lord, which Paul believes to be imminent. The burden of the epistle is detachment, but Paul wants no revolutionary changes in the respective states of life of his readers. Virgins and widows are to remain as they are, following his own example of celibacy. If they cannot remain continent, it is better to marry than to burn with desire (cf. vv. 8.9), a statement, which, if taken in isolation, would suggest that marriage is nothing more than a concession to weakness. However, Paul insists that Christians can be saved in whatever legitimate state their baptism found them. (vv. 17–24) Whence the conclusion: "Are you bound to a wife? Do not seek to be freed. Are you freed from a wife? Do not seek a wife. But if you take a wife, you have not sinned. And if a virgin marries, she has not sinned." (vv. 27.28) The celibate and virginal state is more detached and free from care than the married, says Paul, since a husband is concerned about pleasing his wife and a wife about pleasing her husband; the unmarried are more concerned about the things of the Lord, that they may be holy in body and spirit. (Cf. vv. 32–35.)

The obligations of Christian spouses are clear: each has the right over the body of the other and neither may defraud the other of this right except for a time and by consent, in order that they may give themselves less distractedly to prayer; but they are to resume marital relations lest Satan tempt them for lack of self-control (vv. 3–6). It is Paul's counsel that the unmarried and virgins remain as they are, but "to those who are married, not I, but the Lord commands that a wife is not to depart from her husband, and if she departs, that she is to remain unmarried or be reconciled to her husband. And let not a husband put away his wife." (vv. 10.11)

Death frees the widow and the widower from the bonds of marriage, and they are free to remarry "in the Lord," i.e., to marry a Christian. But it would be better if they remained in the state of widowhood. (vv. 39–40) Somewhat later and as the result of painful experience, Paul changes his advice with respect to young widows: "I desire therefore that the younger widows marry, bear children, rule their households, and give the adversary no occasion for abusing us." (1 Tim 5,14 and context)

With regard to marriages which were entered before the conversion of one or other of the parties, Paul gives the general advice that the Christian should not separate from the pagan partner, since the believer can sanctify the unbeliever. "But if the unbeliever departs, let him depart. For a brother or sister is not under bondage in such cases, but God has called us in peace." (vv. 12–15) Although Paul does not expressly state that the believer is free to remarry after the departure of the unbeliever, Christian tradition will see in the expression "not under bondage" freedom from the bonds of marriage which would otherwise preclude a second marriage. This type of expression is found in Rom 7,2.3, where Paul states: "For the married woman is bound by the law while her husband is alive; but if her husband die, she is set free from the law of the husband." In this instance the woman is free to remarry. Similarly, the Christian deserted by an unbeliever, or married to one who refuses to live at peace with the believer, is no longer bound by the law which forbids remarriage. Such is the interpretation given by the Church today to what has come to be called the Pauline privilege, a privilege either introduced by Paul under divine guidance or promulgated by Paul as the teaching of Christ.

EPH 5 In the epistle to the Ephesians the mood of Paul changes as the *parousía* seems more distant. With the imminent coming of the Lord, Paul had regarded marriage as an obstacle to piety and a distraction from the things of the Lord, an insight which is always valid when the state of marriage is compared with the state of virginity. But in Ephesians Paul expresses the equally valid truth that human love is compatible with love of God, that the former can be the symbol of the latter, the latter the ideal of the former. This concept reaches its peak in Paul's exhortation that "husbands love your wives, just as Christ loved the Church" (v. 25), and that "wives be subject to their husbands as to the Lord; because a husband is head of the wife, just as Christ is head of the Church, being himself savior of the body." (v. 23)

Marriage, then, is not something sheerly natural and profane. It was designed from the beginning as the mysterious symbol of Christ's union with his spouse the Church. As such it has always been sacred. Insofar as it makes of Christians new demands in love and obedience which are supernatural and not merely natural, it is understandable why Christian tradition will come to see in the marriage of Christians not only a sacred symbol of Christ's union with the Church, but an efficacious sign or sacrament of that supernatural love which makes Christ one body with his Church. All this is suggested, as the Council of Trent will affirm, in the passage from Ephesians which reaches its climax in Paul's conclusion: "This is a great mystery—I mean in reference to Christ and to the Church." (v. 32)

## EARLY CONTROVERSIES

The Church was faced from the beginning with a difficult task. Against the Gnostics and the Manicheans who regarded marriage as evil she had to uphold marriage as good and even sacred. Against the Jovinians who regarded marriage as better than virginity, she had to uphold the preeminence of virginity. In attempting to steer a middle course between these two extremes, it is not surprising that some of the Fathers, particularly St. Jerome, so exaggerated the evil of concupiscence as to cast doubt on the ethical goodness of intercourse itself. It has always been difficult to praise something without disparaging its alternative. The wonder of history is that the Church from the beginning succeeded as well as she did in striking a happy balance in her attitude toward the two states, that of virginity and that of marriage, and that she eventually came to proclaim marriage not only as something good and sacred but as a sacrament of the New Law.

### *Gnosticism and Manicheism*

The Gnostics of the second century and the Manicheans of the succeeding centuries regarded matter and the flesh as evil, the emanation of an evil principle, irrevocably opposed to the spirit or soul, the emanation or spark from the good principle. Marriage, since it perpetuates the soul in the prison-house of the flesh, is evil and must not be permitted the true Gnostic or Manichean. Second class Manicheans, however, may marry, but they must avoid conception, which is the work of Satan or the principle of evil. Such in brief is the ethical teaching of the Gnostic sects and the Manicheans in their repudiation of marriage.

It would seem that Gnosticism grew up with Christianity itself, and it is quite possible that St. Paul has an incipient Gnosticism in mind when he warns Timothy:

> Now the Spirit expressly says that in after times some will depart from the faith, giving heed to deceitful spirits and doctrines of devils, speaking lies hypocritically, and having their consciences branded. They will forbid marriage, and will enjoin abstinence from food which God has created to be partaken of with thanksgiving by the faithful and by those who know the truth. For every creature of God is good, and nothing is to be rejected that is accepted with thanksgiving. For it is sanctified by the word of God and prayer." (1 Tim 4,1–5)

St. Irenaeus, writing in the second half of the second century, describes the Gnostic followers of Saturninus and Marcion as Encratites or Continents who "preached against marriage, thus setting aside the original creation of God, and indirectly blaming him who made the male and the female for the procreation of the human race." (*Against Heresies,* 1,26,1) A century later, St. Hippolytus of Rome regards the Encratites as Cynics rather than Christians: "They pass their time inflated with pride; thinking they can gain distinction by dieting, they abstain from animal food, are water drinkers, and, forbidding marriage, they devote the rest of their life to habits of asceticism." (*Refutation of All Heresies,* 8,20) By the close of the fourth century, the Encratites have broken up into a number of small sects, particularly in the East. St. Epiphanius caustically remarks, "If marriage is an unholy thing, then they are either doomed to speedy extinction, or else they must be born out of wedlock." (*Against Heresies,* 61,1)

There has been a tendency among non-Catholic writers to identify the asceticism of these early Encratites with the genuine Christian attitude toward marriage and the other good things of God's creation. Unquestionably there is a surface resemblance between the Encratite and the genuinely Christian ascetic, but the motives that prompted each to forego marriage, meat, wine, and property are wholly different. The difference is spelled out by St. Epiphanius: "The Church praises renunciation, but she does not condemn marriage; she preaches poverty, but does not inveigh against those who possess property. . . . Many in the Church abstain from certain kinds of food, but do not look with contempt on those who do not abstain." (*Ibid.,* 61,2)

In the West, the Encratites are more identified with the Manicheans, or at least with the more ascetic among them. Their basic tenet that marriage is evil and that conception is the handiwork of Satan was condemned at the Council of Braga, a city of modern Portugal, in the year 561. (Cf. D234,241,242.) The ablest defender of the Church's position against the Manicheans was St. Augustine who had been a member of the sect for some eight years before his conversion. However, in turning from the Manicheans to combat the claims of the Pelagians, Augustine is not altogether free from pessimism in his outlook on marriage, and, more particularly, on the marriage act. (See p. 92.)

### *Montanism*

As a Catholic, Tertullian penned what is perhaps the most beautiful tribute to Christian marriage, "which the Church arranges, the Sacrifice strengthens, upon which the blessing sets a seal, at which the angels are present as witnesses, and to which the Father gives his consent." (*To His Wife,* 8) It is Tertullian too who stresses the symbolism of the "great sacrament" as a sign of Christ's permanent love for his Church. (*On Monogamy,* 5) After his deflection to Montanism, however, the latent puritanism in Tertullian comes to the fore and leads him not only to condemn marriages of widows and widowers as a species of adultery but to regard marriage, as such, as a concession to weakness and an evil at best tolerated by God. Ignoring the general teaching of St. Paul and the context of the passage, "It is better for a man not to touch a woman" (1 Cor 7,1), Tertullian concludes: "Therefore it is bad to touch one. For nothing is opposed to the 'good' except the 'bad.'" (*On Monogamy,* 3) Puritanism of the Tertullian variety was condemned at the Council of Nicaea in 325. (D55)

### *Pelagianism and the Augustinian Synthesis*

The Pelagians denied that man's nature was in any way corrupted as the result of Adam's sin. What Catholics called concupiscence they declared to be not only natural to man but also native to Adam and present in Christ, the Second Adam. When it is used in marriage it is a cause of joy; when indulged outside of marriage it is a cause of sin; when completely controlled in the celibate and virginal state it is a cause of triumph. (Cf. the semi-Pelagian work *The Predestined,* 3,31.) Against the Pelagians St. Augustine argued that concupiscence, a part of which is the lustful tendency within us, is the result of original sin.

lust

While not a sin in itself, concupiscence is the evil concomitant of every act of intercourse. Because of this evil there have to be other values to justify sexual intercourse, values which are to be found *in* marriage and which make marriage and the marriage act good. In this context Augustine develops the threefold good of marriage which has become classical: offspring, fidelity, and sacramental sign which stands for permanence of marriage (*proles, fides, sacramentum*). To engage in the marriage act for the sake of offspring is to be free from all blame. To seek the act in order to gratify lust or concupiscence is always sinful, although venially so in those who have pledged their fidelity in marriage. In other words, marriage and the marriage act are good, but to be free from all blame the marriage act must be prompted by sentiments of paternity and not by concupiscence or lust. Marriage, for Augustine, is admittedly a remedy against fornication, but it is in no sense an outlet for pent up sexual desires. (Cf. *On Marriage and Concupiscence, passim.*)

In teaching that concupiscence is the result of sin, Augustine is theologically correct. In teaching that the marriage act must have spiritual overtones to free the act of all blame, Augustine is psychologically sound. In holding, however, that every marriage act must be prompted by hope of offspring, Augustine is overly rigorous. On this point Catholic teaching is better reflected in the encyclical *Casti Connubii* ("On Christian Marriage") par. 59:

> For in matrimony, as well as in the use of the matrimonial rights, there are also secondary ends, such as mutual aid, the cultivating of mutual love, and the quieting of concupiscence, which husband and wife are not forbidden to consider so long as they are subordinated to the primary end, and so long as the intrinsic nature of the act is preserved.

By subordination to the primary end, which is the child, Catholic moralists today understand simply that the marriage act must be performed in a natural way, whether there is hope of offspring or not. As to the sense in which the marriage act "quiets" concupiscence or acts as a remedy for concupiscence, see p. 103.

## MARRIAGE AS A SACRAMENT

### *Early Background*



Against the Gnostics, the Manicheans, and the early puritans, the Church was called upon to defend marriage as one of the good things of God's creation. In the course of this defense the Church insisted that marriage was not only good but sacred. God's blessing on marriage is recorded in the opening hymn of the sacred Books, on creation. Christ by his presence at the marriage feast of Cana not only changed water into wine but transformed human marriage into a union that is sacred and in some sense a source of grace. Thus, St. Epiphanius finds a twofold symbolism in the change of water into wine, a sign that "the turbulent waters of passion are absorbed and restrained by the dignity of marriage, and that, for the future, passion should yield to the refreshing sense of well being which results from the sweet wine of grace (*cháritos*)." (*Against Heresies,* 51,30)

Because of this sacred character of marriage after Christ's coming, the Church from the beginning expected her members to have their marriage blessed by the bishop, and to have their consent solemnized within the context of the eucharistic liturgy. Just as the other sacraments were celebrated in conjunction with the eucharist, so too a place was found for marriage in what has come to be known as the nuptial Mass. (See Tertullian's description, p. 91.) True, there is no direct statement that marriage is a sacrament in the sense that the marriage ceremony confers grace in virtue of the rite performed (*ex opere operato.*) Nor did the Fathers of the Church expressly state that Christian marriage is an efficacious symbol of Christ's love for his Church. The "great sacrament" of Paul was more usually interpreted to refer to the permanence of Christian marriage rather than to its sacramental nature. Yet St. Augustine comes close to asserting that marriage is a sacrament in the strict sense of the word when he likens the permanence of marriage to the permanence of baptism and order, sacraments which imprint an indelible character and hence are not to be repeated. (*On the Good of Marriage,* 28)

### *The Scholastic Period and the Council of Lyons II*

In the twelfth century marriage was included among the seven sacraments distinctive of the New Law. Nonetheless, neither Peter Abelard nor Peter Lombard could bring themselves to believe that marriage conferred grace as did the other six. Neither could see in marriage anything heroic that would merit the reward of grace. Peter Lombard did admit, however, that marriage was a remedy for concupiscence, an admission which led St. Thomas in his commentary on Lombard to conclude: "But concupiscence is not repressed except through grace.



genious)

Therefore grace is conferred in marriage." (*Suppl.*, 52,3) The teaching of St. Thomas was the common teaching of the great scholastic doctors of the thirteenth century. At the reunion Council of Lyons II (1275), a profession of faith in the seven sacraments, marriage included, was drawn up for the Greek Church and accepted by the emperor Michael Palaeologus and the Patriarch Beccos as representative of their own traditions (Cf. D465.) The fact that Orthodox Christians of the East, Russian as well as Greek, recognize marriage as one of their seven sacraments or mysteries is confirmatory proof that marriage was always regarded as a distinctively sacramental rite in the tradition that is common to the East and to the West.

## *The Reformation and Trent*

In his *Babylonian Captivity* written in 1520 Luther denied that marriage was a sacrament. He maintained that the mystery or sacrament of which Paul spoke was not that of marriage but the mystery of Christ's union with his Church. This view is tenable if one uses the Latin of the Vulgate "*in Christo et in ecclesia*" (in Christ and the Church) but unlikely and contrary to Christian tradition if one considers the original Greek "*eis Christòn kai eis tēn Ecclēsían*" (in reference to Christ and the Church.) Ten years later in his treatise *On Matrimonial Affairs* (*Von Ehesachen*), Luther justified his refusal to get involved in marriage legislation by stating: "No one can deny that marriage is an external, secular affair, such as clothing and food, home and real property, subject to secular supervision." (*Luthers Werke,* Weimar ed., 30,3,205) Although most of the reformers, Luther included, were willing to clothe marriage with some religious ceremony, they were all agreed that marriage was not so sacred as to warrant its regulation by the Church.

Reacting against Luther's naturalistic attitude toward marriage and defending the rights of the Church to legislate for Christian marriage, the Fathers of Trent enacted a series of decrees and canons which touch the present matter. They are found in the 24th Session, Nov. 11, 1563, and may be summarized as follows:

(1) Christ merited the grace of marriage which perfects the natural love between husband and wife, strengthens their union, and sanctifies the married couple. This is suggested by St. Paul in the passage from Ephesians which concludes with the statement "This is a great mystery—I mean in reference to Christ and the Church." (Eph 5,32) This same truth is confirmed by Christian tradition. (Cf. D970)

(2) Marriage is truly and properly a sacrament of the New Law instituted by Christ, and it confers grace. (Can. 1, D971)

(3) Marriage cases pertain to ecclesiastical judges. (Can. 12, D982)

Since Luther had attacked clerical celibacy and religious profession, the Fathers of the Council anathematized anyone who would say "that the married state is to be preferred to the state of virginity or celibacy, and that it is not better and more blessed to remain in the state of virginity or celibacy than it is to be united in marriage." (Can. 10, D980) Other points of Trent's teaching will be recorded when we consider the properties of Christian marriage.

## SACRAMENT AND CONTRACT

### *The Marriage Contract*

Although once disputed by the canon lawyers of the twelfth and thirteenth centuries, it is the certain teaching of the Church today that marriage is essentially constituted by the mutual exchange of consent between the two parties. This consent is not merely a promise to marry, an engagement or betrothal (*consensus de futuro*), but an agreement to be married here and now (*consensus de praesenti*). The object of this consent or contract is the exclusive and permanent right over the body of the other party in view of such acts which tend of themselves toward procreation. (*Code of Canon Law*, Can. 1081) Although the essential object of the contract is the right to have intercourse, the marriage contract necessarily includes the right of spouses to each other's love and affection, which will take in the right and obligation to live together, and to afford mutual assistance. These secondary rights, while in the strictest sense not essential to the validity of the contract, stem from it and underline that marriage is not merely the mutual surrender by two of their bodies but of their whole persons. Husband and wife belong to each other.

### *Conditions for a Valid and Lawful Contract*

To contract a valid marriage, the parties must have the actual use of reason and, unless otherwise dispensed, be free from those invalidating impediments which are listed in the *Code of Canon Law*. (Can. 1057–1080) They may be listed briefly: (1) age: sixteen years for the man, fourteen for the woman; (2) impotence (not sterility), antecedent and perpetual; (3) bond of a previous marriage which has not been legitimately dissolved; (4) disparity of cult (marriage with one unbaptized); (5) major orders (including the subdiaconate); (6) solemn religious profession; (7) abduction, so long as the one abducted is in the power of the abductor; (8) crime, either adultery with the promise to marry, or conjugicide; (9) public propriety (*honestas*); consanguinity in the direct line resulting from children born of an invalid marriage or concubinage; (10) consanguinity and affinity, whether in the direct line or, within certain degrees, in the collateral line; (11) spiritual parentage, resulting from sponsorship at baptism; (12) legal parentage, resulting from adoption, where the civil law regards such parentage as invalidating marriage.

Besides freedom from the above mentioned impediments, those who have been baptized in the Catholic Church are held to form, that is, marriage before a priest as the principal witness, provided a priest is available. (Can. 1094) If a priest is not readily available, a marriage celebrated before two witnesses is valid and lawful where there is danger of death or where it is foreseen that a priest will not be available for the space of a month. (Can. 1098)

Besides the impediments which nullify a marriage, there are other impediments which make the marriage unlawful or sinful, unless a dispensation is granted. These are: (1) simple vows; (2) legal parentage, where the civil law forbids the marriage but does not invalidate it; (3) mixed religion, a marriage with a baptized Christian who belongs to a Christian confession separated from Rome.

It should be noted that a dispensation from the impediments of disparity of cult and of mixed religion will not be granted unless the non-Catholic party agrees to respect the faith of the Catholic party and to bring up all children born of the union in the Catholic religion.

### *The Essential Rite of Marriage*

The Council of Trent defined that marriage is a sacrament, but it did not determine the essential rite of marriage. Some theologians believed that the rite of marriage consisted in the blessing of the priest, a view which is not consistent with Trent's teaching that clandestine marriages (marriages not celebrated before a priest) are valid and lawful, so long as the Church regards them as such. (Cf. D990–992) During the sixteenth and seventeenth centuries, the French regalists and the Austrian Josephists, anxious to hand over the regulation of the marriage contract to civil society, distinguished between marriage as a civil contract and marriage as a sacrament. Borrowing a page from Luther, and abetted by theologians who were more loyal to the state than to the Church, the regalists and the Josephists decided that the Church could arrange for the religious ceremony or sacrament while the state would control the contract. The Church replied by insisting that the marriage contract between two baptized Christians is the sacrament of marriage; so much so, that it is impossible for two Christians to enter a valid marriage without the marriage being, by that very fact, a sacrament. The blessing of the priest is not part of the essential rite in the Church of the West, but an accompanying ceremony which is not required for validity. (Cf. *Syllabus of Errors* of Pius IX, D1776, and encyclical letter of Pius XI, *Casti Connubii,* n. 39.) Accordingly, if we are to look for the matter and form of the sacramental rite of marriage, it must be found in the mutual consent of the contracting parties. According to one view, the mutual surrender that is made in marriage is the matter of the sacrament, while the mutual acceptance is its form. All is expressed in the simple response to the priest's inquiry, "I do" or "I will."

### *The Ministers of the Sacrament*

Since sacrament and contract are identified in a marriage between two baptized Christians, the contracting parties are the ministers of the sacrament. The priest is present as the principal witness and as the minister of the blessing, which is a sacramental and not part of the sacrament. Bride and groom are the ministers of grace to each other. As ministers of a sacrament, they must have the intention of conferring the sacrament upon each other, an intention which need not be explicit but is always implicit in the serious exchange of their consent to marriage. Thus, even non-Catholics who are baptized and who do not realize that marriage is a sacrament, administer the sacrament to each other provided they intend a valid marriage. "There can be no true marriage between baptized persons without its being by that very fact a sacrament." (*CIC*, Can. 1012)

## THE BOND OF MARRIAGE

The immediate effect of the marriage contract or sacrament is the marriage bond, an entity in the juridical order which unites husband and wife until death. The bond is also an entity in the physical order, a kind of character uniting husband and wife in a special relationship with the mystical body of Christ, in which and through which the sacramental grace of marriage is received. As a physical or ontological reality we can refer to the bond as the *res et sacramentum* of marriage, the symbolic reality of marriage. The bond is the first effect of marriage, antecedent by nature to grace and yet disposing husband and wife for the reception of grace if no obstacle is put in the way. In this sense the bond is the sign that makes ready for grace (*signum dispositivum*). But it is also a sign which configures or likens the soul of the husband to Christ as groom and the soul of the wife to the Church as bride of Christ (*signum configurativum*). Their union is the sign or sacrament of Christ's union with his Church. As such it will have the same properties as the union between Christ and his Church. That union is one and indissoluble. There is but one Church of Christ; one Church alone is his bride. Christ's union with his Church will last until the death of this world and the final summing up of all things in Christ.

### *Properties of the Marriage Bond*

A consummated Christian marriage alone symbolizes in full the permanence and exclusiveness of Christ's union with his Church, since such a marriage cannot be dissolved even by the Church. And yet in restoring marriage to its primitive dignity as the exclusive and permanent union between a man and a woman, Christ prescribed for all marriage, non-Christian as well as Christian. His immediate concern was the Jewish practice of a man's divorcing his wife and remarrying, but his words: "What God has joined together let no man put asunder," has application not only to the Hebrew male. Every male and female, and, according to Catholic teaching, all human authority, including the authority of the state, are subject to this prescription, in virtue of its source. Accordingly, marriage is not only intrinsically indissoluble—it cannot be terminated at the will of the contracting parties; it is also extrinsically indissoluble—it cannot be terminated by the intervention of the state or civil society.

Some marriages, it should be noted, can be dissolved by the Church with an authority which is not human but vicariously divine. The authority spoken of is that vested in Peter and the Twelve, and continued in Peter's successors: "Whatsoever you shall loose on earth shall be loosed in heaven," an authority which has application to the loosing of the bonds of sin, and, according to Catholic tradition, an authority which has application to certain types of marriages.

As already noted, Christ did not directly touch the matter of polygamy which is opposed to the unity of the marriage bond. However, in teaching that a man does commit adultery against a woman, he asserted the basic marital rights of a woman which are violated whether the husband divorces her or brings another woman into his home. (See p. 84.) Against this scriptural background we can briefly study the practice and teaching of the Church on the unity and indissolubility of the marriage bond.

### *Unity of the Bond*

So foreign to Christian thinking was polygamy, whether through a plurality of wives (polygamy) or a plurality of husbands (polyandry), that many bishops of the early Church permitted second marriages of widows and widowers with extreme reluctance. In the East the digamist and the trigamist (one who entered upon a second or third marriage after the death of one's spouse), were often subjected to severe penalties, even though their marriages were regarded as valid. The first Christian to question the exclusiveness of Christian marriage on theological grounds was Martin Luther, who felt that the dispensation supposedly granted the Jewish patriarchs could have application to Philip of Hesse, whose political loyalty Luther was courting at the time. Luther's action in allowing Philip to take a second wife probably influenced the Fathers of Trent in anathematizing anyone who would say "that it is licit for Christians to have many wives at the same time." (Can. 2; D972)

### *Indissolubility of the Bond*

For the first five centuries the Church of the East as well as the Church of the West was irrevocably opposed to divorce for whatever reason. In fact there is no clear proof that the Church allowed remarriage even in cases where the conditions for the Pauline privilege were verifiable. With the breakdown of the Roman Empire, the Church of the East gradually came to tolerate the lax marriage legislation of the Eastern emperors. The Code of Justinian, which allowed divorce for a variety of reasons besides adultery, was adopted in practice by Eastern bishops and has remained normative in the schismatical Orthodox Churches to this day.

In the West, the Christian ideal of indissolubility rose and fell with the respect or disregard in which clerical celibacy was held. During the eighth and tenth centuries the Frankish Church was in desperate need of reform. The state of the clergy was deplorable, both intellectually and morally. In such a climate it is understandable that at least two local synods, that of Vernon-sur-Seine and that of Compiegne, should tolerate divorce and remarriage for a variety of reasons. In the ninth century an attempt at reform was made under the emperor Charlemagne but the reform did not last long. It was not until the close of the eleventh century and under the leadership of Pope Gregory VII (Hildebrand) that effective legislation was introduced to rule out divorce and to reform the morals of the clergy. From the time of Hildebrand the indissolubility of Christian marriage was recognized universally in Western Christendom up until the time of the new "reform" instituted by Martin Luther.

In keeping with his strong naturalistic tendencies, which regarded celibacy as morally impossible for the clergy, Luther believed that the Church's laws on divorce were too severe, particularly those which forbade the remarriage of the innocent party in the case of adultery or desertion. (*Babylonian Captivity,* 5, "Marriage") Luther's solution was to allow civil society to determine the grounds for divorce and remarriage, in accord with his general principle that marriage, like other sheerly temporal matters, was to be regulated by the state.

Against the teaching of Luther the Fathers of Trent defined that marriage cannot be dissolved by one of the spouses on the grounds of heresy, incompatibility, or desertion. (Can. 5; D975) Against the practice of the Greek Orthodox the Fathers of the Council defined that the Church is not in error in teaching that in accord with evangelical doctrine the bonds of marriage cannot be dissolved on the grounds of adultery. (Can. 7; D977) In his encyclical *Casti Connubii,* Pius XI refers to Canon 7 of Trent, and concludes that if marriage cannot be dissolved even in the case of adultery, "it is evident that all other weaker excuses . . . are of no value whatsoever." (n. 89)

## THE GRACE OF MARRIAGE

According to the Council of Trent, the grace of marriage perfects the natural love between husband and wife, strengthens their union, and sanctifies them. (See p. 94.) This sanctification consists essentially in an increase of sanctifying grace and divine charity. The first act of marriage is, then, a twofold act, an act of mutual love expressed in the contract, and an act of mutual sanctification. Bride and groom are not only lovers. Sharing through baptism in the priesthood of Christ, and acting as Christ's ministers of the sacrament, they give grace to each other. Their first and best wedding gift is the gift of grace. Since marriage is a sacrament of the living, the recipients of the sacrament should already be alive with the life of grace. However, if one or the other of the parties is in serious sin, and a priest is not available for confession, it is generally agreed that imperfect contrition (attrition) by one in good faith, together with the sacrament of marriage, will restore the sinner to life. Love of God covers a multitude of sins. In marriage love of one's spouse, so long as there is some sorrow for having offended God, will do the same. Should the one in sin remain attached to sin, his marriage will be valid but unfruitful. Grace will be withheld until he is restored to life through the sacrament of penance or through an act of perfect contrition with the intention of confessing his sins.

Besides sanctifying grace, which is common to all seven sacraments, husband and wife confer on each other gifts and adornments which are peculiar to marriage, and which assist them in living up to the ideal of marriage proposed by St. Paul. These special gifts or graces may be called, together, the sacramental grace of marriage. In his encyclical on Christian Marriage, Pius XI refers to these added gifts as, "dispositions, seeds of grace" which

> elevate the natural powers in such a way that the parties are assisted not only in understanding, but in knowing more intimately, in adhering to firmly, in willing effectively and in successfully putting into practice those things which pertain to the marriage state, its aims and duties.

Besides these habitual gifts and dispositions, Pius XI teaches that marriage gives them "a right to the actual assistance of grace, whenever they may need it for fulfilling the duties of their state." (n. 40)

This right or title to actual grace is something like a blank checkbook which the parties are privileged to fill in as their needs demand. God guarantees to honor the check, provided both parties cooperate with his grace. Many theologians hold, however, that husband and wife must be in the state of grace to retain their right to God's assistance. They must, in other words, keep the wedding gift of grace, which they administered to each other on the day of their marriage. Failure to keep this gift, or failure to recover it immediately if lost, will explain why so many indifferent or fallen away Catholic couples find marriage so insuperable a burden, if they shoulder the burden at all.

## THE PURPOSE OF MARRIAGE

Christian tradition has long distinguished two basic purposes of marriage, the one looking to the good of the race, the other looking to the mutual perfection of husband and wife. Actually the two ends are complementary. For purpose of analysis we shall treat them separately.

*The primary end* of marriage is the procreation and rearing of the child. "Increase and multiply and fill the earth." This end is called primary in the sense that it is the more important. A person must exist before he can develop his personality in or out of marriage; the birth of children is essential for the continuance of the race. The mutual perfecting of husband and wife contributes to the *well-being* of the race. "It is not good for man to be alone." It should be noted however that the child is not the continuation of the race in the abstract. He continues the race only in as much as he continues his parents. In an extended sense we can say that the words "they shall be two in one flesh" is ultimately realized in the child, who is bone of their bone and flesh of their flesh. It is in the child that the union of husband and wife is objectively realized and projected outside themselves.

*The secondary end* of marriage is the mutual help and support of husband and wife and is expressed in many ways: perfect community of life, two-in-oneship, mutual perfection on the physical, emotional, rational, and spiritual planes. It includes the idea of cohabitation, life together, and above all love, since it is by love "that all the other rights and duties of the marriage state must be regulated." (*Casti Connubii*, n. 25)

In recent years there has been a tendency even among some Catholic authors to invert the hierarchy of ends, placing more stress on the mutual perfection of husband and wife than on the more social aspect of marriage as ordered toward the family. Unquestionably the intention of these authors was good. The secondary values of marriage were often regarded as means only to the primary end, procreation, and not as values to be cultivated for their own sake. However the manner of speaking of some of these writers at times ran counter to traditional terminology canonized by the *Code of Canon Law* in the definite statement: "The primary end of marriage is the procreation and education of the child." (Can. 1013)



In a reply of March 29, 1944, the Holy Office condemned those who would deny that procreation is the primary end of marriage, or who teach that the secondary ends are equally primary and independent. (*AAS*, 36 [1944], 103) A happy balance was struck by Pius XII in a special allocution to the judges of the Holy Roman Rota in which the pontiff concluded:

> In short, if truth "stands in the middle," two extremes are to be avoided: on the one hand, practically to deny or unduly to depreciate the secondary purpose of marriage and of the act of generation; on the other, to dissociate or separate unduly the marital act from the primary purpose for which, by the whole of its intrinsic structure, it is primarily and principally intended. (*AAS*, 33 [1944],423)

*The two ends are complementary*. If the full meaning of marriage is to be realized, the social and the more personal values of marriage must be realized together. The good of the race is not fostered simply by multiplication of the species. As Augustine states, and as the encyclical *Casti Connubii* insists, "children should be begotten lovingly and educated religiously" (n. 17); this can only be done where husband and wife strive to realize the secondary purpose of marriage, mutual love and sanctification. Again, the love and the mutual perfecting of husband and wife is in some sense not fully realized unless the love between husband and wife is fruitful in the child. A wife is perfected by becoming a mother, a husband by becoming a father. A childless marriage is in part a frustrated marriage. The first to admit this is the couple in love and yet childless through no fault of their own. There is a tendency among some non-Catholic marriage counsellors to look upon children as an obstacle to love rather than the normal and spontaneous fruit of love. They will counsel young couples to postpone the first child, on the naïve supposition that the child will interfere with the love that husband and wife should have for each other. Actually there is but one love that the child can interfere with, and that is self-love or selfishness. Love by its very definition is a giving of self, a surrender of the self to the beloved to find union. The greatest obstacle to this love is selfishness. Deliberate childlessness is a sign that love was absent at the time of marriage or that it was stifled early in marriage.

*The remedy for concupiscence* is a secondary value of marriage made necessary by the fall of man and the loss of the gift of integrity or wholeness. (See p. 80f.) St. Paul advises that "it is better to marry than to burn [with concupiscence]" (1 Cor. 7,9), and in verse 2 he says "For fear of fornication let each man have his own wife, and let each woman have her own husband." Many authors have interpreted Paul's teaching to mean that marriage is a legitimate outlet for pent up sexual desire which would otherwise find expression outside of marriage. There is, however, a deeper reason why marriage is a remedy for concupiscence. In marriage, the marriage act is more than an outlet for sexual desire. It is or should be the physical expression of the surrender that has already been made on the affective and rational levels, a surrender that has been made in the marriage contract. St. Augustine demanded that the marital act be tempered by sentiments of paternity and fidelity, and in this he was both theologically and psychologically sound. (See p. 92.) The Jesuit moralist, A. Vermeerch, is kin to Augustine when he states that marriage as a remedy for concupiscence "is not well understood if you suppose that concupiscence can be tempered by concupiscence. In marriage the sexual union ennobled and sanctified by the affection of lawful love is substituted for those unions where concupiscence is dominant." (*Theologia Moralis,* 4, n. 41, p. 35)

## MARRIAGE AS A VOCATION

Although virginity and celibacy embraced for the sake of the kingdom of God are more excellent in themselves, marriage is the school of Christian perfection for most men and women. They will be saved and will advance God's kingdom in and through their marriages. Marriage is God's kindly strategy for educating people to a love of benevolence and the virtue of altruism. Upon the latter depends love of God and neighbor, which in turn fulfill "the whole Law and the Prophets." (*Casti Connubii,* n. 23) True, there are many married couples who live their lives in a wholly self-centered fashion. But without being oversanguine we have good reason to believe that most couples, particularly when children come, rise appreciably above the level of selfishness to the heights of benevolence and Christian charity. The Rt. Rev. J. M. Cooper, an eminent anthropologist, feels that it would be safe to say that

> a good ninety percent of the deeds of justice and charity, of fulfillment of the Commandments and of the Works of Mercy, carried out in this human world of ours is carried out within the family and kinship circle. At any rate, we are surely on safe ground in holding that at least most of the love and unselfishness in the world stems directly or indirectly from marriage and family life." ("Charity Begins at Home," in *The Family Today,* NCWC, 1944)



For most people, a more intensive training in altruism begins with marriage. A man and woman may enter marriage impelled in part by any number of reasons: to better their economic or social standing, to satisfy their sexual drives or their desire for companionship, to obtain security, all self-regarding motives. Once married, however, most husbands and wives find themselves in conditions that constitute forceful incentives for awakening the play of the unselfish elements in marital love. As time goes on and husbands and wives are continued in sons and daughters, the field of love widens. Further demands are made on their selflessness, demands which are frequently accepted as a matter of course, and where love is of finer quality, even joyously.

Charity begins at home, but if it is true charity, it cannot end there. Love is by definition diffusive of self. True love, unless nature intervenes—and this is the great tragedy of a husband and wife in love—will become fruitful in children. Normally, the love of husband and wife will build itself a home that is full of children, and yet large enough for the neighbors' children. It will build itself a table, but never too small for an extra plate. It will build itself a door that is wide enough for the poor and the outcast to enter in. It will fashion within the husband and wife hearts expansive enough to embrace the world and, ultimately, God himself. For the ultimate purpose of marriage, like the ultimate destiny of man himself, is the knowledge and love of God in the beatific vision.

A SUPPLEMENT

# THE RELIGIOUS LIFE

The ascent of love, from love of self to love of another in marriage and ultimately to the love of God, is the means by which the majority of men and women work out their salvation. The state of marriage, however, is not the only way or, absolutely speaking, the most perfect way for man to achieve his final destiny. Virginity and celibacy in preference to marriage, and widowhood in preference to second marriage, for those who are called to these states, have an ancient and honorable history in the Church. Human love can lead to a love that is divine, but it can also be an obstacle to divine love. The path lies open for Christians to love God directly, without the mediatory help of a human lover. In such case they must be on their guard, of course, against the hindrance provided by their own persons, unchallenged as they will be by the demands of love in a family situation.

Christ praises the detachment of those who sever all family ties, and promises a special reward in this life and in the life to come to those who "have left house, or parents, or brothers, or wife, or children for the sake of the kingdom of God." (Lk 18,30) In the same chapter of Matthew's gospel in which Christ upholds the ideal of celibacy for the kingdom of heaven's sake (Mt 19,12), he offers the rich young man a life that is more perfect than the simple fulfillment of the commandments: "If you will be perfect, go sell what you have, and give to the poor, and you shall have treasure in heaven; and come follow me." (Mt 19,21)

In the early Church, many young Christians endeavored to follow Christ by embracing the ideal of perfect continence and poverty. The men among them entered the clerical state and fostered the ideal of clerical celibacy. The women either dedicated themselves to God privately or consecrated themselves to God as virgins in a ceremony which seems to have been modeled on the appointment of widows and deaconesses. (See p. 63.) At first these consecrated virgins did not live in community, but a place of honor was reserved for them along with the widows during the celebration of the liturgy. Not living in community they made no special vow of obedience to a superior.

During the period of persecutions, Origen (c. 250) lists in order those whose self-oblation as living victims is especially pleasing to God. The first in order after the apostles is the martyr, and the second is the virgin or the celibate, and the third are the married, who are not to be denied the privilege of offering their bodies as a victim holy and pleasing to God. (Cf. *On Romans,* 9,1.) After the period of persecutions (315), when it was no longer possible to give one's life for Christ in the martyr's witness, the life of the evangelical counsels was embraced by many as a substitute for martyrdom.

In the East many Christians, encouraged by the heroic example of St. Antony (c. 315), went off to the desert to lead the life of the hermit or solitary. As a result, however, of the influence of St. Pachomius and St. Basil in the East, and St. Benedict in the West, the life of the hermit yielded in great part to the life of the cenobite, i.e., the monk or nun living in community and obedient to a fixed rule and to a superior. Thus, the religious life as we know it today developed in the monastic orders of men and women, in the groups of clergy who lived a common life and by rule ("canons"), and in the later congregations of priests, brothers, and sisters. Characteristic of all these religious communities are the three vows of poverty, chastity, and obedience. In the religious orders, these vows are solemn. They have the effect of dissolving the marriage bond if the marriage has not been consummated. Again, solemn profession is a diriment or invalidating impediment to marriage. In the later religious congregations the vows taken are simple, both temporary and final. Yet the surrender to Christ made in both simple and solemn vows is the same in its spirit if not in its effects. It is an heroic witness to the highest Christian ideal, a surrender which, with God's grace, overcomes the triple desire inbred in fallen man: "the lust of the eyes," by the vow of poverty, "the lust of the flesh," by the vow of chastity, and "the pride of life," by the vow of obedience. (Cf. 1 Jn 2,16.)

Martin Luther rejected the ideal of the religious life, not merely as too demanding on him but as unnatural for all. (See p. 74.) But as the non-Catholic educator F. W. Foerster observes in a chapter happily entitled, "The Indispensability of the Ascetical Ideal":

> If the compulsion of nature be so urgent, how can one demand continence before marriage? In fact how can one demand a chaste life from the unmarried? . . . Celibacy is not a merely hierarchical institution, as has been assumed, but it is at the same time an institution in favor of family life, a heroic taking of the offensive against the confident power of merely natural impulses—which make more and more demands the more concessions one makes to them, and whose despotism can be broken only by renunciation on the great scale. (*Marriage and the Sex Problem* [New York: Stokes, 1936], pp. 154f)

# *Selected Readings*


## PART ONE

Galtier, Paul, *Sin and Penance* (St. Louis: B. Herder, 1932).

Lubac, Henri de, *Catholicism* (New York: Sheed and Ward, 1958), Ch. III, "The Sacraments."

McNeill, J., and H. M. Gamer, *Medieval Handbooks of Penance* (New York: Columbia University Press, 1938).

Palmer, Paul F., *Sources of Christian Theology*, Vol. II: *Sacraments and Forgiveness. History and Doctrinal Development of Penance, Extreme Unction and Indulgences* (Westminster, Md.: Newman Press, 1959).

Paulus, Nikolaus, *Indulgences as a Social Factor in the Middle Ages* (New York: Devin-Adair, 1922).

Riga, Peter, *Sin and Penance: Insights into the Mystery of Salvation* (Milwaukee: Bruce, 1962).

Roguet, A. M., *Christ Acts Through Sacraments* (Collegeville, Minnesota: The Liturgical Press, 1954).

## PART TWO

The following papal encyclicals are published by the Paulist Press and the America Press: Pius XI, *Ad Catholici Sacerdotii Fastigium* (On the Christian Priesthood); *Casti Connubii* (On Christian Marriage). Piux XII, *Sacra Virginitas* (On Holy Virginity).

Bligh, John, *Ordination to the Priesthood* (New York: Sheed and Ward, 1956).

Doms, Herbert, *The Meaning of Marriage*. Translated and abridged from the authorized French version by George Sayer (New York: Sheed and Ward, 1939). Despite its overemphasis on the secondary or personal values in marriage, this book is a landmark on the finality of Christian marriage.

Hope, Wingfield, *Life Together* (New York: Sheed and Ward, 1943).

Joyce, George H., *Christian Marriage: An Historical and Doctrinal Study* (New York: Sheed and Ward, 1933).

Leclercq, Jacques, *Marriage and the Family: A Study in Social Philosophy*, 4th ed. (New York: Pustet, 1949).

———, *The Religious Vocation* (New York: P. J. Kenedy and Sons, 1955).

Le Saint, W., and P. Palmer, *Sources of Christian Theology*. Vol. III: *Sacraments and Vocation. History and Doctrinal Development of Priesthood, Celibacy and Marriage* (Westminster, Md.: Newman Press, in preparation).

Levis, Robert W., *The Presentation of the Essentials of Marriage in the College Marriage Course* (microfilmed Ph.D. dissertation, The Catholic University of America, 1963).

Mersch, Emile, *Love, Marriage and Chastity* (New York: Sheed and Ward, 1939).

# ABBREVIATIONS

## *The Books of the Old and New Testaments*

| | | | |
|---|---|---|---|
| Genesis | Gn | Canticle of Canticles | Ct |
| Exodus | Ex | Wisdom | Wis |
| Leviticus | Lv | Sirach (Ecclesiasticus) | Sir |
| Numbers | Nm | Isaia | Is |
| Deuteronomy | Dt | Jeremia | Jer |
| Joshua | Jos | Lamentations | Lam |
| Judges | Jgs | Baruch | Bar |
| Ruth | Ru | Ezechiel | Ez |
| 1 Samuel (1 Kings) | 1 Sm | Daniel | Dn |
| 2 Samuel (2 Kings) | 2 Sm | Osea | Os |
| 1 Kings (3 Kings) | 1 Kgs | Joel | Jl |
| 2 Kings (4 Kings) | 2 Kgs | Amos | Am |
| 1 Chronicles (Paralipomenon) | 1 Chr | Abdia | Abd |
| 2 Chronicles (Paralipomenon) | 2 Chr | Jona | Jon |
| Ezra | Ez | Michea | Mi |
| Nehemia (2 Ezra) | Neh | Nahum | Na |
| Tobia | Tb | Habacuc | Hb |
| Judith | Jdt | Sophonia | So |
| Esther | Est | Aggai | Ag |
| Job | Jb | Zacharia | Za |
| Psalms | Ps(s) | Malachia | Mal |
| Proverbs | Prv | 1 Machabees | 1 Mc |
| Coheleth (Ecclesiastes) | Coh | 2 Machabees | 2 Mc |

In the enumeration of the Psalms, the first number follows the Vulgate, the number within brackets, the Hebrew text.

| | | | |
|---|---|---|---|
| St. Matthew | Mt | 1 Timothy | 1 Tim |
| St. Mark | Mk | 2 Timothy | 2 Tim |
| St. Luke | Lk | Titus | Ti |
| St. John | Jn | Philemon | Phlm |
| Acts of the Apostles | Ac | Hebrews | Heb |
| Romans | Rom | St. James | Jas |
| 1 Corinthians | 1 Cor | 1 St. Peter | 1 Pt |
| 2 Corinthians | 2 Cor | 2 St. Peter | 2 Pt |
| Galatians | Gal | 1 St. John | 1 Jn |
| Ephesians | Eph | 2 St. John | 2 Jn |
| Philippians | Phil | 3 St. John | 3 Jn |
| Colossians | Col | St. Jude | Jude |
| 1 Thessalonians | 1 Thes | Apocalypse | Ap |
| 2 Thessalonians | 2 Thes | | |

## *Apocrypha and Qumrân Material*

| | | | |
|---|---|---|---|
| Henoch | Hen | Testament of the Twelve Patriarchs | Test |
| Jubilees | Jub | | |
| Psalms of Solomon | Ps Sol | Manual of Discipline | MD |

## *Other Source Material*

*Acta Apostolicae Sedis*
[Acts of the Apostolic See] — *AAS*

*Ancient Christian Writers,*
ed. J. Quasten and others — *ACW*

*Acta Sanctae Sedis*
[Acts of the Holy See] — *ASS*

*Codex Iuris Canonici*
[Code of Canon Law] — *CIC*

Denzinger-Bannwart, *Enchiridion Symbolorum,* 30th ed. [Handbook of the Creeds] — D

*Patrologia, series graeca,*
ed. J. P. Migne — *PG*

*Sacrorum Conciliorum nova . . . Collectio* — *Mansi*

*Patrologia, series latina,*
ed. J. P. Migne — *PL*

*Summa contra Gentes*
S. Thomae Aquinatis — *S.C.G.*

*Quatuor Libri Sententiarum,*
Petri Lombardi [Four Books of Opinions] — *Sent.*

*Summa Theologiae*
S. Thomae Aquinatis — *S.Th.*

*Supplementum tertiae partis Summae Theologiae* (Ottawa ed. 1941) — *Suppl.*

*The Church Teaches,*
ed. J. Clarkson and others — *TCT*

# INDEX


## A

Aachen, Council of (836), 47
Abelard, Peter, 22-23, 30, 93
Abimelech, 71
Abraham, 81
Absolution (*See* Penance and Indulgences)
Agar, 81
Albert, Archbishop of Mainz, 74-75
Albert the Great, 48-49
Alcuin of York, 47
Alexander VII, Pope, 33
Alexander VIII, Pope, 31
Ambrose of Milan, Saint, 73
Anselm, Saint, 22
Antony, Saint, 107
Aquinas, Thomas, Saint
  absolution formula, 19
  on extreme unction, 48-49
  on indulgences, 40
  on marriage, 93-94
  on penance, 19, 23-24, 30, 33, 34, 35, 40
  on sacrament of order, 65, 66, 68, 70
Aristotle, 24
Arles, Council of (314), 64
Athanasius, Saint, 20
Attrition, 23, 30, 32-34, 101
Augustine, Saint
  on forgiving and retaining of sins, 8, 36
  on marriage, 86, 91-92, 93, 103, 104
    Augustinian Synthesis, 91-92
  on ordination, 64, 65
  penance, sacramental character of, 20-21
  on priestly celibacy, 73
  on public penitents, 15
Augustinian Synthesis, 91-92

## B

*Baius*, 31
Baptism, sacrament of, 6, 7, 8, 12, 34-35, 36, 37, 43, 44, 50, 64, 68
  baptismal character, 34-35
Barnabas, 59
Basil, Saint, 16, 107

Beccos, Patriarch, 94
Bede, the Venerable, 47
Benedict, Saint, 107
Binding and loosing, formula of, 7-8, 9
Bishops
appointment of presbyter-bishops, 57
monarchical, 62
ordination of, 63
powers of, 67-69
Bonaventure, Saint, 23, 48
Bora, Katherine (wife of Martin Luther), 74
Braga, Council of (561), 91
Bystander, 16

C

Caesarius, Bishop of Arles, 46
Cain, 80
Calvin, John
on extreme unction, 49
on penance, 24, 25-26
on the sacrament of order, 66
Cana, 93
Carolingian reform, 47
*Catechism of the Council of Trent,* 44, 49, 51
Celibacy, priestly, 70, 71-77, 107
Council of Trent on, 74, 75
doctrinal significance, 76-77
early development of, 72-76
in Eastern Orthodox Churches, 75-76
Luther on, 74-75
in the Middle Ages, 74
Charlemagne, 100
Christ
on celibacy, 72
forgiving of sins, 1-3, 6-7
on marriage, 78-79, 82-87, 93
ministry of healing, 2, 43
priesthood of, 56-57
Clement of Alexandria, 12
Clement of Rome, Pope, 11, 57, 61, 62
Clement VI, Pope, 40
Clermont, Council of, 40
Code of Justinian, 99
Confession, 5, 14-15, 28, 37-38
value of, 37-38
Confirmation, 44, 68
Constance, Council of (1415), 65
Constantinople, Council "in Trullo" (692), 75
Continents, 90
Contrition, 5, 17, 23, 27-28, 30, 32-34, 101
contritionist-attritionist controversy, 32-34
differentiated from attrition, 30
Contrition (*Cont.*):
perfect and imperfect, 27-28
putative, 23
Cooper, J. M., 104
Cornelius, Saint (Pope), 13
Council "in Trullo" of Constantinople (692), 75
Council of Aachen (836), 47
Council of Arles (314), 64
Council of Braga (561), 91
Council of Clermont, 40
Council of Constance (1415), 65
Council of Elvira (305), 73, 75
Council of Florence (1439), 66
Council of Jerusalem, 11, 31
Council of the Lateran I (1123), 74
Council of the Lateran II (1139), 74, 75
Council of Lyons II (1274), 31, 65, 94
Council of Mainz (847), 47
Council of Nicaea (325), 13-14, 64, 75, 91
Council of Rome (386), 73
Council of Trent
on extreme unction, 49, 50-51
on hierarchy of order, 55-56
importance of, 30-31
on indulgences, 41
on marriage, 76, 79, 89, 94-95, 96, 99, 100
on penance, 5, 21, 24, 26-31, 34, 36, 51-52
on priestly celibacy, 74, 75
on sacrament of order, 55-56, 60, 65, 67
Cranmer, Thomas, 24, 26
Crusade Indulgence of Urban II, 40
Cynics, 90
Cyprian of Carthage, Saint, 13, 17, 21

D

David, 6, 71
Deacons, ordination of, 57-59
De Wette, 75
Digamist, 99
Divorce, 81-82, 84, 99-100
in ancient Israel, 81-82
Dominic, Saint, 64
Donatism, 64
Donatus, 64
du Bay, Michel (*Baius*), 31

E

Eligius, Bishop of Noyon, 46
Elvira, Council of (305), 73, 75
Encratism, 75

Encratites, 90
Ephesus, 59
Epiphanius, Saint, 90, 93
Eucharistic sacrifice, 57, 69
Eusebius, 12
Excommunication, 7, 8-10
Extreme unction, sacrament of, 1, 42-52
  Code of Canon Law, 52
  Council of Trent on, 49, 50-51
    *Catechism* of, 49, 51
  proper ministers of, 51
  recent contributions, 51-52
  reformers, teaching of, 49-50
  Scholastic speculation, 48-49

F

Florence, Council of (1439), 66
Foerster, F. W., 108
Francis of Assisi, Saint, 64

G

Gelasius, Pope, 10
Gnosticism, 75, 89-91, 92
Gregory the Great, Pope, 17
Gregory VII (Hildebrand), Pope, 74, 100

H

Healing sacraments, 1-3, 44-48
  anointing the sick, 44-48
  apostolic ministry of healing, 43
  blessing oil of the sick, 45
  Christ's ministry of healing, 2, 43
  priestly rite of healing, 43-44
  purpose of, 2
Hearer, 16
Hermas, 12
Hermit, 107
Herod, the Tetrarch, 59
Hildebrand (Gregory VII, Pope), 74, 100
Hillel, 82, 83
Hippolytus, Saint, 45, 47, 62, 90
Holy Roman Rota, 103
Hugh of St. Cher, 40
Hugh of St. Victor, 22-23
Hus, John, 65

I

Ignatius of Antioch, Saint, 57, 62
Indulgences, 31, 39-41
Indulgences (*Cont.*):
  absolution grants, 39-40
  Council of Trent on, 41
  defined, 39
Innocent I, Pope, 17, 46
Innocent III, Pope, 65
Irenaeus, Saint (Bishop of Lyons), 12, 90

J

James, Saint, 43, 44, 46, 47
Jansen, Cornelius (*Jansenius*), 31
Jansenist movement, 31-32, 33
Jerome, Saint, 85, 89
Jerusalem, Council of, 11, 31
Jesus (*See* Christ)
Jezebel, 10, 11
John (Saint), 6, 7, 10, 11, 62, 83
John, the Evangelist, 12
Jovinians, 89
Jubilee Bull of 1343, 40
Justinian, Code of, 99

K

Kleist, J., 62

L

Lamech, 80
Lateran, first Council of (1123), 74
Lateran, second Council of (1139), 74, 75
Lennerz, H., 69
Leo the Great, Pope, 15, 18, 21
Leo X, Pope, 24
Leo XIII, Pope, 68, 81
Lombard, Peter, 22-23, 48, 93
Lord's supper, 50, 57, 66
Lucius of Cyrene, 59
Luke, 2, 83, 84
Luther, Martin
  on extreme unction, 49
  on marriage, 94-95, 99
  on penance, 24-25
  on priestly celibacy, 74
  on the religious life, 107
  on the sacrament of order, 66
Lyons, Council of (1274), 31, 65
Lyons, Council of (1275), 93-94

M

Mainz, Council of (847), 47
Malachia, 82

Manahen, 59
Manicheism, 89-91, 92
Marcion, 90
Marcus, the Gnostic, 12
Mark, 2, 83, 84
Marriage, sacrament of, 78-105 (*See also* Vocation, sacraments of)
  in ancient Israel, 80-82, 98
    divorce, 81-82
    Mosaic legislation, 81-82
    polygamy, 80-81
  the bond of marriage, 97-100
    indissolubility of, 99-100
    properties of, 98-99
    unity of, 99
  Christ's teachings, 78-79, 82-87, 93
  Council of Trent on, 89
  divine institution and purpose, 79
  divorce, 81-82, 84, 99-100
  early controversies, 89-92
    the Augustinian Synthesis, 91-92
    Gnosticism, 89-91
    Manicheism, 89-91
    Montanism, 91
    Pelagianism, 91-92
  essential rite of marriage, 96-97
  and the fall of man, 80
  the grace of marriage, 100-101
  the marriage contract, 95-96
  marriage as a sacrament, 92-96, 99, 100
    Council of Lyons (1275), 93-94
    the Council of Trent, 94-95, 96, 99, 100
    the Reformation, 94-95
  marriage as a vocation, 104-105
  ministers of the sacrament, 97
  Pauline privilege, 99
  polygamy, 80-81, 82, 84, 85, 99
  purpose of marriage, 102-103
  teachings of St. Paul, 87-89
Matthew, 83, 84, 85, 106
Maximilla, 12
Michael Palaeologus, Emperor, 31, 65, 94
Montanism, 12-13, 14, 63-64, 91
Montanus, 12
Moses, 69, 71, 81-82
Mourner, 16, 17


## N


Nathan, the prophet, 6
Nicaea, Council of (325), 13-14, 64, 75, 91
Nicanor, 58
Nicholas, 58
Niger (Simon), 59
Noah, 80
Novatian, 13, 20
Novatianism, 13
Novatus of Carthage, 13


## O


Order, sacrament of, 55-77, 107 (*See also* Vocation, sacraments of)
  Anglican orders, 68
  apostles, priesthood of, 57
  Barnabas, ordination of, 59
  bishops, ordination of, 63
  charismatic ministry, 60-61
  compared with sacrament of baptism, 64
  the Council of Trent on, 55-56, 60, 65, 67
  deacons, ordination of, 57-59, 63
    rite of ordination, 58
  early heresies, 63-64
    Donatism, 64
    Montanism, 63-64
  grace of order, 68, 70
  hierarchy of orders, 55-56
  Hippolytus, ordination rites of, 62-63
  matter and form of orders, 68
  in the Middle Ages, 64-66
    revival of heresies, 64-65
    Scholasticism, 65
  orders, development of, 61-63
    monarchical bishop, 62
    sacrificial priesthood, 61-62
  power of order, 68-70
  presbyter-bishops, appointment of, 59
  priesthood of Christ, 56-57
  priestly celibacy, 70, 71-77, 107
  reformers, teaching of, 66-67
  rites of ordination, development of, 66
  Saul, ordination of, 59
  Timothy, ordination of, 59-60
Origen, 46, 107


## P


Pachomius, Saint, 107
Palaeologus (*See* Michael Palaeologus, Emperor)
Paphnucius, Bishop, 75
Parmenas, 58
Paul, Saint
  on excommunication and reconciliation, 8-9
  forgiving sins, 7
  on marriage, 85, 87-89, 90, 91, 94, 101, 103-104
  on penance, 11, 13

Paul, Saint (*Cont.*):
  on the sacrament of order, 58, 59-60, 61
Pauline privilege, 99
Paulus, N., 41
Pelagianism, 91-92
Penance, sacrament of, 1, 5-41, 42, 44, 46, 51-52, 101
  absolution formula, 19, 22, 28
  absolving action of priest, 5, 22-23, 28
  acts of penitent, 5, 27
  apostolic ministry of forgiveness, 7-9, 22
    formula of binding and loosing, 7-8, 9
    formula of forgiving and retaining sins, 7, 8, 9
    "power of the keys," 8, 22-23
  attrition, 23, 30, 32-34, 101
  belief of the early Church, 19-21
  Celtic discipline, 18-19
  Christ's ministry of forgiveness, 6-7
  confession, 5, 14-15, 28, 37-38
  continental discipline, 18, 19
  contrition, 5, 17, 23, 27-28, 30, 32-34, 101
    differentiated from attrition, 30
    perfect and imperfect, 27-28
    putative, 23
  contritionist-attritionist controversy, 32-34
  the Council of Trent, 5, 21, 24, 26-31, 34, 36, 51-52
  early controversies, 11-14
  early discipline, 14-18
  effects of, 34-38
  excommunication, 7, 8-10
  Jansenist movement, 31-32, 33
  the Orthodox Churches, 31
  matter (*quasi*) and form of, 24, 27
  necessity of, 21,, 27
  as a sacrament, 20-21
  sacramental grace of, 37
  reconciliation, 8-10, 17-18, 46
  the Reformation, 24-26
  reviviscence of merits, 37
  role of the Church in matter of sins, 7
  satisfaction, 5, 29-30
  Scholastic teaching on, 22-24
  sin of final impenitence, 10
  symbolic reality, 34-36
  unpardonable sins, 9-10
  value of confessions of devotion, 37-38
Peter, Saint, 8, 11, 20, 72, 98
Philip, 58, 59
Philip of Hesse, 99
Pius V, Saint (Pope), 41
Pius XI, Pope, 52, 78, 81, 101
Pius XII, Pope, 38, 68, 70, 103
Polyandry, 99
Polycarp, Saint, 11
Polygamy, 80-81, 82, 84, 85, 99
"Power of the keys," 8, 22-23
Priesthood (*See also* Order, sacrament of; Celibacy, priestly)
  absolving sins, 5
  of the apostles, 57
  celibacy, 70, 71-77, 107
  of Christ, 56-57
  power to confirm or ordain, 69
  priestly rite of healing, 43-44
  the religious life, 106-108
  sacrificial, 61-62
Prisca, 12
Prochorus, 58
Protestant Reformation (*See* Reformation)

## R

Recidivist, 14
Reconciliation, 8-10, 17-18, 46
Reformation (*See also* Luther, Martin; Calvin, John)
  on extreme unction, 49-50
  on indulgences, 41
  on marriage as a sacrament, 94-95
  on penance, 24-26
  on the sacrament of order, 66-67
Religious life, 106-108
Rome, Council of (386), 73

## S

Sara (wife of Abraham), 81
Satisfaction, 5, 29-30
Saturninus, 90
Saul, 59
Scholasticism (*See also* Aquinas, Thomas, Saint; Abelard, Peter; Lombard, Peter)
  on extreme unction, 48-49
  on marriage as a sacrament, 93-94
  on penance, 22-24
  on the sacrament of order, 65
Scotus, 24, 48
Serapion, Saint, 45
Shammai, 82, 83, 85
Simon (Niger), 59
Sins (*See* Penance, sacrament of)
Siricius, Saint (Pope), 16, 73
Sixtus IV, Pope, 40
Socrates, 75

Sozomen, 15
Stephen, 58-59
Symbolic reality, 34-36

T

Tertullian of Carthage, 13, 14, 19-20, 46, 63-64, 91, 93
Thomas, Saint (*See* Aquinas, Thomas, Saint)
Timon, 58
Timothy, 57, 59-60, 70, 72, 90
Titus, 72
Trent, Council of (*See* Council of Trent)
Trigamist, 99

U

Urban II, Pope, 40

V

Vermeerch, A., 104
Vocation, sacraments of, 53-54 (*See also* Order, sacrament of; Marriage, sacrament of)
von Harnack, A., 61

W

Waldensians, 64-65
Waldo, Peter, 65
William of Auvergne, 23
Wycliffe, John, 65